BOOK

"Dr. Daniene Marciano, in her debut novel, has cleverly interwoven the preparation of Italian food into the intellectual, artistic refinement and traditions of the Italian culture during the late nineteenth and early twentieth centuries. The events leading up to their trip to America and while on the ship were gravely challenging and nearly unbearable.." Linda Serfina, Editor, California.

* * * * *

"A loving presentation of early Italian culture with a "feel good" plot. This is a land mark read." Susan Jones, Director in Florida

* * * * *

"Desperate for a more productive and prosperous life, the Triolo family endures countless, riveting hardships to start a better life in the new world." Valentina Opizzi, Project Manager in Silicon Valley

* * * * *

"Pillars of a Legacy: An Italian Experience is a brilliant story that captures the essence of the tragedies and hardships of the Sicilian Italians and their flight to America for a better life." Leonardo De Marco, CEO in Wisconsin

* * * * *

"This book, Pillars of a Legacy: An Italian Experience, is a unique story of three generations of Sicilian families in the nineteenth and twentieth centuries. Hard to put the book down!" Gabriele Pagnotto, Business Owner in Florida

* * * * *

"A fantastical story that has many twists and turns. Very interesting!" Liliana Ricci, Retired Administrative Assistant in California

* * * * *

"Fresh, dangerous, exciting events in Palermo, Corleone, Sicily and America in the late 1800's and the beginning of the 1900's." Adalberto Auriemma, CFO in Colorado

* * * * *

PILLARS OF A LEGACY:
AN ITALIAN EXPERIENCE

BY DR. DANIENE MARCIANO

First published by Dog Ear Publishing
4011 Vincennes Rd
Indianapolis, IN 46268
www.dogearpublishing.net

ISBN: 978-1-4575-6173-3

This book is printed on acid-free paper.

Printed in the United States of America

DEDICATION

TO MY BABY GIRL, PRINCESS, MY CHERISHED PUPPY

I am crying now as much as I was rejoicing when I brought you home in my arms thirteen years ago. Bravery was one of your strongest qualities. You rode on the airplane across the country, all alone, to get to our home. So itsy-bitsy, yet in your gentle, beautiful eyes, I saw such an enormous capacity for love.

My beloved, incredible puppy, you were so sweet and regal in your quiet ways. A perfect guardian, you were the most faithful companion. For two years, you sat at my feet while I was writing this book. You somehow knew how important it was for me to do.

Your ancestors came from Malta, hence, your Maltese breed. Only just recently I discovered that some of my ancestors came from Malta, too. Perhaps this is one of the reasons for our bond.

You will be forever remembered, forever missed, and forever in my heart. There will only be one you. I have loved you beyond all feelings; I have missed you with grief beyond all tears.

I look forward to our joyous reunion, so I can feel, once more, your happy rain of kisses on my face.

Princess with author
For gorgeous classic cars, see:
bill@checkeredflagclassics.com

"Life is not about waiting for the storms to pass but rather how to dance in the rain."
—Vivian Greene

SOMMARIO (TABLE OF CONTENTS)

OLD WORLD CHARACTERS

Francesco Triolo	Antonino's father, husband of Anna
Anna (Monteleone) Triolo	Antonino's mother, wife of Francesco
Cardinal Alberto Cusimano	Pope's selection committee, Giovanna's uncle
Bishop Giorgio Lucchessi	Pope's selection committee
Father Guido Primo	Local Sicilian priest, Pope's selection committee
Bruno Lorenzo	Lifelong friend of Francesco and Anna, father of Vincenzo Lorenzo
Josephina Lorenzo	Wife of Bruno, mother of Vincenzo
Guglielmo Soracco	Lifelong friend of Francesco and Anna
Maria (Margherita) Soracco	Lifelong friend of Francesco and Anna
Luciano Margherita	Father of Maria
Sebastiana Margherita	Mother of Maria
Pellegrino Margherita	Brother of Maria
Niccollo Albanesi	Mayor of Corleone
Roberto Provenza	Military general
Deanno Graziano	Captain of boat going to Rome
Vito Sangeovese	Military strategist for the Triad

Digger	Miner, blackmailer, trouble-maker
Mirella Margherita	Friend of Guglielmo Soracco
Isabella	Mother of Giovanna, wife of Alessandro
Alessandro	Father of Giovanna, husband of Isabella

Central characters are based on real people. The primary characters are deceased. Other important characters are composites of real people or are invented. Many of the events and dates are true and accurate, but certain liberties have been taken with many names, places, and dates.

NEW WORLD CHARACTERS

Antonino Triolo, leader	Son of Francesco and Anna
Giovanna (Cusimano) Triolo, teacher	Wife of Antonino
Vincenzo Lorenzo, priest	Lifelong friend of Antonino and Giovanna
Daniele Soracco, doctor	Lifelong friend of Antonino and Giovanna
Rosina (Quattrone) Soracco, nurse	Wife of Daniele
Marcello Scardino	Captain of the SS *Vincenzo Florio*
Maximiliano Fortunati	Mafia member, "Mad Dog"
Fabio Testi	Woodsman, father of Edoardo, Stefano, and Pietro
Giullietta Mondadi	Betrothed to Robert Smith
Robert Smith	Chief of the Police Jury Commission
Placido	Organizer, surveyor
Nunzio	Butcher
Cuncetta	Wife of Nunzio
Giuseppe	Baker and fisherman, father of Sophia
Paolo Nero	Carpenter
Angelina	Passenger on the ship, wife of Giuseppe
Benito Deotto	Gold leaf artist
Dario Conti	Wood craftsman
Remo Remotti	Organ builder, musician

Preface

In 2012, my husband and I took a monthlong Mediterranean cruise. One of our destinations was Sicily; in fact, it was the last destination on our itinerary. I believe the cruise planners saved the best for last. Prior to visiting Italy, I had always dreamed of going to Sicily and discovering if we still had relatives there.

As we disembarked, I was both nervous and excited about what possibilities might exist in my great-grandfather's and great-grandmother's revered Corleone. The fluttering in my stomach increased as we set foot on the beloved shores of Palermo.

We approached a taxi service and requested to be taken to Corleone. Eyebrows went up when we announced our destination. Even today there exists an aura of trepidation surrounding Corleone, the birthplace of the Mafia. We were too enraptured in our quest to find members of the Triolo family to give much thought to unfounded anguish. Our request was to have an English- and Italian-speaking driver. The drivers did not compete for the assignment because of where we were going.

Our driver, also our interpreter, was fun-loving and anxious to help us. Of all the handsome men in Italy, the Sicilian men are the most gorgeous. He shared some history with us as we drove along the winding road. It was a warm, clear day, and I kept anxiously hoping that I would be reunited with my relatives.

The terraced hills reminded me of Tuscany. The flora and fauna were rich, verdant, and profuse. I knew that every turn would bring me closer to where my relatives had lived. It was almost inconceivable that 150 years ago my progenitors walked the same roads that I was about to walk.

Our first stop was at the hall of records to locate more information about my family. An officious woman greeted us. She stood grandly with her head up, back straight, eyes flashing and hands folded within each other. It was obvious that she was in charge. Our driver explained to her why we were there. She referred us to a short, stodgy lady sitting at a desk.

Another conversation ensued and the lady at the desk nodded her head to indicate that she understood her responsibility. She put on her glasses, stood up, and walked over to the library.

The room held shelves upon shelves housing large, old, dusty books. Shifting up and down, walking her fingers across each sacred book, she searched for the dates I had given her. Her fingers came to a halt; she leaned and reached for the book. Dust flew everywhere while she teetered back and forth, attempting to balance herself with the large book.

She plopped the book on her desk, causing me to cough and sneeze from the cloud of dust that arose. She took off her glasses and set them squarely on her workstation while she lunged for a container that had another pair of glasses hidden inside. She promptly put the new pair on and opened the tome.

With a magnifying glass and her finger to guide her, she carefully looked at every name and date. I was getting more and more excited as she searched. After a few moments, she dramatically stopped and smiled. She had found my great-grandfather's dates, along with my great-grandmother's and their children's.

Next, the librarian took out a pad of paper and pen to write down her discoveries. She slammed the book closed and rose to return it to its rightful place. Again, she bobbed up and down to find another book that provided information about my grandfather and grandmother.

When she had completed her task, she handed me the piece of paper. On it, she had written down all the salient points of my ancestors. I received the document with trembling hands and tears running down my face. To make me even more emotional, she told our driver that she knew Antonino Triolo (my great-grandfather) and that he lived very close to where we were.

I was confused. *How could this be?* Antonino had lived well over a century ago, yet his address was listed. I could not control my tears. I raised such a ruckus that six ladies came out of their offices, plus the woman in charge. I hugged the librarian, and then all the Italian women lined up for me to hug them too! Italians love to hug. They were so happy for me. Even the straight-backed lady wanted a hug.

We left the building in search of Antonino's residence. Our first stop was where four older Italian men were talking with their hands. The driver asked them for directions. They pointed us where we needed to go.

After circling around a number of streets, we saw a similar group of older Italian men on the corner talking with their hands. The same question was asked and they pointed us in the opposite direction given to us by the first group of men. What an adventure!

While driving in the newly designated area, I yelled to the driver, "Stop!" His tires screeched to a halt. At the dead end of one of the streets was a large official poster on the wall asking people to vote for a gentleman with the last name of "Triolo" for President. I could not believe my eyes.

After going a circuitous route, we came to the store where, upstairs, Antonino supposedly lived. We went into the store and asked for Antonino. The sales manager nodded her head yes and pointed upstairs. We waited for her to call him on the old-fashioned, black dialer phone. It rang and there was no answer. I was so disappointed.

The sales manager advised us to wait for him. In the meantime, we walked down the street and came to a house with the same address the librarian had given us. It had a cyclone fence around it and was under construction. A sign revealed that Antonino Triolo was, indeed, the owner of this house. It said that the house had ten rooms, but it did not delineate what the rooms were.

It was my great-grandparents' house from so long ago. It had been built with the living quarters upstairs and a breezeway downstairs. In the nineteenth century, when the Triolos lived there, the roofed outdoor passage under the house was where all the cows, pigs, and other livestock slept. It was now being converted into a garage.

We took plenty of pictures with me hugging and kissing the building. We then went back to the store and asked the sales lady to phone Antonino again. The phone rang on and on, but there was still no answer. I was crestfallen.

We were getting ready to leave when I heard the lady shout something in Italian. She was saying that Antonino had just arrived in front of the store. As Antonino opened his car door, the lady ran to him, saying that his cousin was visiting from America.

He had the largest smile on his face as he ran in to meet me. Not speaking a word of English, he repeated over and over again, "*mia famiglia*" ("my family") to me. We embraced and kissed on the cheek. My husband knew some Italian and asked Antonino to lunch with us. He graciously accepted.

Having grown up in Corleone, he knew the best restaurant. We drove per his instructions while Antonino and I held hands. He was so strikingly handsome. No one would guess that he was eighty-four years old. He had silver wavy hair, and very blue, radiant eyes, which surprised me. He was trim and muscular and stood about five feet, eight inches. His eyes twinkled as he grinned.

As we traveled, he shared that he had been a first-grade teacher all his working life. I was elated that he shared that profession with me. I said that I was an instructor at the University of California, Berkeley. He knew about the university and was happy that I had also been a teacher of all grades and an administrator for many years. What a coincidence!

He had never married, so he had no children. I told him I could hardly believe that some woman had not proposed to such a dapper gentleman. He laughed and his blue eyes glimmered. At that moment, we arrived at the hilltop, open-air restaurant. The driver was fortunate to be a part of our group. He ate more than anyone and took the leftovers home!

Antonino introduced us to his friends, the restaurant owner and his wife, and ordered the food. In a matter of minutes, we had a huge *antipasti* dish in front of us. Everything was incredibly fresh and delicious. Before we could finish, waiters were bringing out enormous shrimp on a decorative platter. We enjoyed the feast, looking out over the terraced hills. It was then that Antonino and I determined that we were fourth cousins once removed.

The staff knew when to bring out each platter and what wine to pair with our courses. Our favorite wines were *Valdicava Brunello Riserva Madonna del Piano* and *Amarone della Valpolicella* consisting of *Corvina, Rondinella,* and *Molinara grapes*.

We had beef, then pork, then lamb. All arrived on colossal platters. Grilled and roasted vegetables were served intermittently. Delicate pastas were offered to us: raviolis, gnocchi, cannelloni, and rigatoni with our choice of tomato, Alfredo, or pesto sauces.

The salad is always served as the last course in Italy. *Chi mangia bene, vive bene* (Who eats well, lives well!).

By then, it was difficult to breathe because we were so full. As we strained to eat the salad, Antonino borrowed the owners' mandolin, and he began singing beautiful Italian songs.

He asked the owner's wife if he would play music for the *tarantella* ("tarantula") dance when he finished singing. It was in Naples that this dance was invented and it spread quickly to other Italian regions.

Antonino offered his hand to me while we whirled, skipped, and held our arms up high, doing the tarantella. He was a masterful dancer and I followed his lead. We'd had enough wine to make dancing easy. All the while we danced, he repeated *"mia famiglia,"* and kissed both my hands. As we whirled, it was as though I was in a magical dream.

It was an experience that I never expected, nor even imagined as perfectly as it happened. When it was time for us to drop Antonino off and return to our ship, we both cried as we embraced once more. As we began to drive away, he shouted, *"mia famiglia"* throwing a kiss into the air.

I left a changed person. As a result of my journey, I had a personal connection with my ancestors, experiencing happiness, anger, sadness, and too many other emotions to describe. Antonino and I are kindred spirits.

ACKNOWLEDGEMENTS

I would like to acknowledge my extraordinary parents, Daniel George Parle, and Maria (Mary) Ann Triolo. They requested that I write a book depicting the history of both sides of our family coming to America. One side of the family is from Sicily, Italy, and the other is from Ireland. My Irish story is forthcoming.

Papa Parle and Mamma Triolo

Additionally, I want to acknowledge my most wonderful and caring Triolo aunts and uncles: Anna, Antonio (Tony), Josephine, Francesco (Frank), and Leo Luca (Luke).

Top, left to right: Antonio, Francesco, and Leo Lucca
Bottom, left to right: Anna, Josephine, and Maria

I wish to recognize my supportive husband, William Sr., for encouraging me to pursue this endeavor, and my amazing and truly awesome sons, William Jr. and Sam, for their esteeming admiration while enjoying all of my adventures.

It is with sadness that I thank my dear first cousin, Genevieve, who is deceased. She worked tirelessly compiling the Triolo genealogy. Her children, Carrie and Brice, preserved her work.

Also, this book was written for all of my Triolo cousins, especially my dear Antonino, who lives in Palermo, Corleone, Sicily, today.

I am beholden to my entire family and friends, especially the "Fun Bunch," who shared Italian stories and motivated me to continue writing about this exceptional journey.

CHAPTER 1

POWER AND CONTROL

In 1816, Naples and Sicily were united to form the "Kingdom of Two Sicilies." They had two kings: Charles of Anjou, King of Naples, and Peter of Aragon, King of Sicily. After Charles' army attacked Sicily, he became the ruler of both lands. His reign was viewed as an enlightened time in history and the beginning of a golden age. Naples became a metropolis and the richest city in the Italian states were under his rule.

Many advances were made during Charles' reign. A two percent salary deduction funded the first labor pension system. Public housing was institutionalized, and, besides the regular school system, the first school for the deaf was built. Taxes were the lowest they had been in years. Printing presses were abundant. In Naples, the famous opera house, *Teatro* (Theater) di San Carlo, was erected. Palaces were constructed. Naples was among the first cities to install a gas street lighting system. Metalworks, glass, and porcelain production were encouraged, to improve industry. The biggest iron and steel manufacturing as well as casting foundries, were expanded. The two regions had the largest steamships in the Mediterranean.

Charles' grandson, Ferdinand I, created the largest army in the Italian states. The fact that sulfur was plentiful for making gunpowder and medicine contributed to his power.

Desiring a liberal government for twenty years since the 1840s, Italian intellectuals and agitators had caused riots against the Bourbons' declining economy and conservative rule. Powerful, independent city-states with regional loyalties erupted. From a time of peace, order, and progress, utter chaos abounded. Ferdinand's son, Francesco II, did nothing to stop revolutionaries such as Giuseppe Garibaldi, who seized Sicily and Naples in 1860 with his followers, known as the "Red Shirts," and the country became independent of foreign rule.

Some Sicilians owned their own home and at least a parcel of land. That year, the Catholic Church and landowners with large land holdings distributed property to the peasants. Authorities did not settle land disputes, so the landowners needed someone to arbitrate their arguments. Innocently, landowners hired paralegals to protect their interests. Opportunists struck, and the Mafia was born. The Mafia collected payments for "protecting" the landowners from each other. With more property owners came more disputes that needed settling and more properties that needed to be "protected" from neighboring interests. What had started as a legal and just system became a nightmare, as the arbitrators saw the great potential for extortion and joined forces with the Mafia to take advantage of the landowners. Greed spread quickly throughout the paralegals. They knew the property owners were desperate to keep their holdings safe from other landowners and criminals.

Even church-owned lands were seized. Church schools shut down. Illiteracy soared. The press was censored.

Moderate taxes became exorbitant. Disputes over land escalated. Southern Italy became poverty stricken, rural, and socially backward, a fertile environment for organized crime. Unemployment contributed to the evolution of the Mafia, because being a part of it was lucrative. Ultimately, it led to unimaginable crime and murder.

In 1861, Garibaldi forced the controversial unification of all the Italian city-states, known as "Risorgimento." This action created further havoc, especially in southern Italy.

The new country's constitution supported northern Italy and persecuted the south, especially the island of Sicily, off southern Italy. Crushing taxes were applied to southern Italy and Sicily. The northern area was exempt from taxes, so it had the opportunity to become cosmopolitan, to flourish, and to urbanize.

Western Sicily at this time, especially Palermo, a well-established port, was more prosperous than the other provinces, providing more opportunities for racketeering and extortion. The eastern part of the island was poor and had fewer lawbreakers. Salt field owners, citrus orchard owners, cattle ranchers, and sulfur entrepreneurs were targets of crime because they were wealthy. Most of the population of the southern area and Sicily consisted of craftspeople, small landowners, sharecroppers, and agricultural laborers.

By 1861, there were eight powerful Mafia clans; consequently, the innocent Triolo, Lorenzo, Soracco (the Triad), and Cusimano families were among those that were beleaguered by these monsters.

The 1862 massacre began the *Cosa Nostra* ("Our Thing") Mafia's long history of abominable deeds. People wouldn't give up money or property. They'd take it by force, then, or at least petrify landowners into submission. A "boss" or "don," along with a *"consigliere"* (advisor, usually a lawyer) ran a Mafia clan. All orders came from the don. Structured below them was the "underboss," who took care of things if the boss was away, occupied with something else, or dead. The "underboss" conveyed the order to three *"caporegimes"* ("sergeants"). They gave orders to the "soldiers," who carried out the orders from the don, no matter how barbaric. One started in this life at the bottom of the bureaucracy by being an associate, who was below even the soldiers. They had to work their way up the chain of command to be boss by obediently performing the unspeakable tasks that were expected of them.

By 1870, immigration to America became more popular for Sicilians than the Italian mainlanders. The second large Mafia attack occurred in 1899. The reason was the same. Criminals wanted more money, more power, and more property. The battles were on Corleone soil, the capital of Sicily, to force the survivors into submission. Thereafter, the Mafia was deeply rooted into the community.

The fate of Sicily was the backdrop of a deep and enduring love affair between Francesco Triolo and Anna Monteleone. Their son, Antonino, was destined to do miraculous things.

CHAPTER 2

SURVIVAL

The 1899 attack was swift. Smoke danced a macabre dirge, and the stink of sulfur permeated the air. Dusty gunpowder encapsulated the area. Children cried as they looked for their parents.

Soon after the battle was over, uninjured Sicilians helped the dead and wounded, carrying the dead to their church for a proper Roman Catholic burial or to the hospital. Francesco Triolo, just seventeen, had been spared in the attack that had taken his parents. Not knowing what else to do, he joined the helpers. Even from an extremely young age, Francesco was empathetic, and he had wisdom not expected in a young man. His mother used to tell him that he had a lion heart, one that allowed him to be brave and have insight into others' pain or their joy.

An injured Anna Monteleone, sixteen and likewise orphaned, her home seized by Mafia men, lay in the sludge, clinging to life. Fortunately, Francesco noticed her angelic face, even though it was now covered with silt and blood. Normally, her dark blonde hair made ringlets around her oval face and hazel eyes. He knelt down, realized she was still alive, and hurried her off to the hospital; scooped in his arms, his nearly six-foot frame enabling large, determined strides.

At the hospital, doctors and nurses gently cleaned her wounds as she lay moaning in pain. Anna was given laudanum, an alcoholic tincture of 10 percent opium fla-vored with cinnamon or saffron. She passed out from such a strong concoction, so Francesco started to leave for another run to see who else he could find.

In the chaos, a traumatized patient screamed. He grabbed Francesco's arm as he was passing by his bed.

"Help me! Help me! Don't leave!"

"What can I do?" Francesco asked. As he moved in closer, he noticed that the fighter had lost half of his left leg. The doctors gave him belladonna, another painkiller.

After viewing the injury, Francesco believed that the patient was injured in the battle because someone gave him the "evil eye," the "*malocchio*" (mal = evil, and occhio = eye). The remedy for the evil eye is the *cornicello* (cornetto, or little horn) amulet, a bull's horn, which symbolizes the bull's victory over his enemy. Ideally, it should be given to someone as a gift. Fashioned in a crooked horn, the *cornicello* is used to protect against one's enemy or bad influ-ences. Also, the horn can bring many blessings, such as luck, success, and wealth.

"Please find my wife. I do not know what happened to her during the battle. Her name is Josephina Lorenzo."

"I will do my best to find her, sir. What is your name?"

"Bruno Lorenzo."

"It's nice to meet you. I am Francesco Triolo."

With that promise, Francesco left the room. He wanted to remember to tell Josephina, when he found her, to give a "little horn" to Bruno.

He went to one of the doctors and recounted the sol-dier's story. The kind doctor told Francesco to go and see the *sindaco* (mayor), Niccollo Albanesi, the next day. He was trying to reunite families who had been separated during the attack.

Back home that night, so many scenarios of the soldier's wife rushed through his mind as he fell asleep. *Would he be able to find her? Was she still alive? Was she in pain from wounds? Was she tormented because she couldn't find her husband? Did she have children to protect? Was their home still intact?*

The next morning, after a breakfast of "eggs in purgatory," he was ready to fulfill his promise to the fighter. As he waited in the waiting area, people came and went from the mayor's office. Some cried and some smiled, so he felt a little nervous waiting for the magistrate. The assistant finally escorted him into the mayor's office after a lengthy wait.

The mayor stood up from his chair and smiled to greet him. He was self-assured and serious. Authority came naturally to this tall man. He stood very straight, confidently. Some might have said that he was arrogant or narcissistic, yet Francesco was impressed with his relaxed, friendly demeanor when he sat down. Niccollo looked straight into his eyes, which made him squirm a little.

The mayor began, "I understand that you are here to help a victim in the hospital find his wife."

Francesco was startled; he did not expect Mr. Albanesi to know each individual case.

"Yes," he said. "His name is Bruno Lorenzo, and his wife is Josephina Lorenzo; sadly, he lost half of his left leg."

"I see," said the mayor. "I can refer you to several groups: besides the group helping in the hospital, one is cooking for the injured inside the church's hall and one is washing all the clothes. They are at the river. I would advise you to search those areas. When you know what her circumstances are, come back here to let me know."

"Yes, sir, I will."

How helpful he was, thought Francesco. The stories that he had heard about the mayor, that he was commanding and untrustworthy, did not fit his perception of him. Francesco ran to the church and began asking if anyone knew Josephina Lorenzo. The responses were not encouraging. Finally, he approached the pastor and asked him the same question.

Father said, "I know her, but I do not know where she is."

Francesco thanked the holy man. He would have to journey to the river. It was Monday, so he would have to scramble. If one were to start a journey on a Tuesday or Friday, the superstition goes, it would end in a disaster.

He traveled home to grab some fresh vegetables from his garden and the rest of the stale bread. Next, he had to borrow a horse. His neighbor had one by the name of Pokey. He wouldn't make it there quickly, but he left with a hopeful heart. It was midday, so he would arrive at the river late in the day, probably too late to find anyone washing. Later that night, he devoured his dinner. It had been a long time since breakfast. When finished, he tied up the horse and laid a blanket down on the ground to sleep. He woke with birds chirping and a rooster crowing in the distance.

His heart pounded and his fingers tingled in hopes that Josephina would be washing clothes with the other ladies. He suddenly saw a black cat cross his path. He had to backtrack and find another way to the river to avoid crossing the cat's path, which would bring him bad luck.

At midmorning, the first lady he saw was on her knees slamming wet clothes against the rocks.

"Excuse me, but I am looking for Josephina Lorenzo. Do you know her, or do you know where she is?"

The woman silently shook her head from side to side. Another lady approached him.

"She is deaf," the lady said to him. "The School for the Deaf released people to help us."

Francesco was familiar with the school, because he had volunteered to help there many times.

"Do you know a lady by the name of Josephina Lorenzo? I am searching for her to reunite with her wounded husband."

The lady went along the riverfront asking Francesco's question. "No, no, no," resonated. Francesco could hardly believe that no one knew her. Downhearted, he set out for home.

He traveled a different route home than he had come, just in case he came across anyone new to ask about Josephina.

The road had a bridge that dated back to the Roman Empire. Pokey's hoofs clattered on the stone as he crossed. As he reached the bank on the other side, he heard men below talking about their prisoners. He stopped Pokey. *Josephina, a prisoner?* That possibility had not crossed his mind.

He was not safe in this part of the country, near where battles were fought. He looked down and could see what was happening. There were seventeen prisoners, an unlucky number.

Traveling to the left side of a hill, he could see the prisoners a little better, and there were three women in the group. Some captives were either sitting on the ground or sleeping on it; the alert ones were listening to what the kidnappers were saying about what they would do with all of them.

Then, they all began arguing. Should they be killed, tortured for information on property that could be confiscated, or traded for something they wanted from the mayor? Suddenly, a short, heavy-set man, referred to as "Machine Gun," quelled their arguing; he said he would let them know the next morning.

Francesco prodded Pokey to run as fast he could to the mayor, but it took many hours. Pokey was exhausted, thirsty, and hungry when they arrived. Excitedly, Francesco shared the story with the mayor. Mr. Albanesi called the troops to action, put General Roberto Provenza in charge, and gave Francesco a strong, speedy horse. Francesco led the way. Thirty men followed. It took only a few hours to arrive near the prison camp.

About a mile from their destination, they stopped to discuss the plan of attack. General Provenza wanted them to initiate a surprise, evening charge. Everyone tied up his horse, except the scouts. They were to go to the site and return with an update on what was happening in the camp.

The rest of them brought out some food. Darkness came after their dinner. By that time, the scouts had returned with the news that they saw only four captors. The general explained how to assault the camp. Half of the men would go left around the hill, and the other half right. On the general's command, they were to besiege the kidnappers. The general's goal was to have as few deaths or wounded as possible.

The order sounded. They struck quickly, and the skirmish lasted only a few minutes. The four criminals were tied up and the prisoners released. The rest of the enemy troops were not far from the site, so the general made sure they left immediately. There was no time to ask for Josephina Lorenzo. Francesco prayed that she was in the group of captives. The restrained prisoners rode double on the rescuers' horses. Several hours later, they stopped for a respite to eat quickly. Within minutes, they were on their horses again, heading to Corleone.

The scouts went ahead and informed the mayor that they were coming home. When the ragtag group arrived, the mayor and the townspeople greeted them with a cheer. The general and Francesco dismounted.

"Congratulations to our gallant rescuers," Mayor Niccollo called out and asked for a status report.

General Provenza praised Francesco for his bravery and leadership. Provenza reported no deaths.

Francesco finally was able to ask if Josephina Lorenzo was in the rescued crowd and explained about finding her husband at the hospital. Her name echoed down the line. He had just about given up when a frail, petite lady stepped out of line to answer to the name of Josephina. Francesco couldn't believe his eyes. He had accidentally found her in a place he never imagined her to be. The mayor observed Josephina starting to cry with joy.

Francesco escorted her to the hospital; he suggested that she provide a *cornicello* for Bruno, hoping for good luck. She agreed. Francesco did not have the heart to tell Josephina about her husband's injuries; he wanted the doctor to do that. She began calling Bruno's name, getting louder as she reiterated the call. The nurses had to hush her because many of the patients were sleeping.

Francesco found Bruno deeply sleeping, so they both waited for him to awake. Several hours had passed, and Bruno was still sleeping, so they went for a short walk to refresh themselves. As they returned to the hospital, Josephina heard her name called out. She looked around the area and saw the daughter of her best friend.

"Why are you here, Anna? You are so pale."

One of the side effects of her painkiller was a pallid complexion, like someone with tuberculosis. She described how she was injured when the combatants attacked. Her father and mother were killed right before her eyes, but she escaped. Josephina had sustained a number of injuries and fainted. That was when the captors found her.

She introduced them. "Anna Monteleone, this is Francesco Triolo."

Blushing, Anna said, "Francesco carried me to the hospital."

"What a coincidence! Francesco rescued me, too, from the Mafia."

Josephina turned around to give Francesco a smile. Her eyes were small and deep in their sockets. She looked weary from her ordeal. Dried leaves stuck out of her messy brunette hair, and her clothes were dirty and wrinkled from sleeping on the ground. Still, Anna was so happy to see her.

"Your parents, my husband, you, and I were all hurt or killed at the same battle," Josephina remarked.

Bruno had not awakened yet, but she felt the need to excuse herself to be with him. She promised that she would come to visit Anna again. Francesco looked back at her when they left, and Anna was watching his every move.

Josephina went to sit by Bruno's side while Francesco beckoned the doctor. Bruno woke up when he heard his wife's voice. Thankfully, the doctor was there at the same time. Josephina cried hysterically with the news that he lost his leg. She worried for his health, as well as their future life. Francesco's heart ached at the site of both of them crying. He left, to give them time together.

On the way out, he passed the captivating Anna, but she was sound asleep. He looked closely at her, to take in her beauty. Yes, as she slept, she looked like an angel.

Francesco went home exhausted, making sure that his shoes or other clothing were not left on his bed to bring bad luck, and poured himself into bed.

CHAPTER 3

KINDNESS

The next day, Josephina and Francesco went back to visit Bruno and Anna in the hospital. Josephina remembered to bring a *cornetto* amulet to Bruno. Every day Francesco would go to Josephina's and walk her to the hospital after work. One day, Francesco nervously handed Anna a bouquet of flowers; then, he gave her a *cornetto*. She was so happy receiving the gifts, especially the good luck charm. She immediately put the necklace around her neck.

Josephina went ahead to see her husband. She still did not know how she and Bruno, given his injuries, could make enough money for food and shelter after he was released from the hospital.

She left Bruno when he fell asleep and went to visit Francesco and Anna. Josephina knew that Anna had nowhere to go when she was released from the hospital, because her family was dead. As a single woman, Anna could not live on her own, as Francesco, a single man, could. Tradition dictated that she live with a family until she married. A betrothal for marriage had already been decided for her, but the families involved had been murdered.

Josephina knew that Anna was skilled in gourmet cooking and sewing. If Anna consented to live with the couple, she could help earn money in exchange for room and board.

Anna was astounded. Without hesitation, she said, "Yes. I would love to live with you. My mother loved you, and I know that she is smiling down from heaven now. I will cook, clean, and sew to help you and Bruno."

This idea made Francesco happy, too. Josephina and Bruno lived near the meadow, which was not too far from where he lived with his family.

His betrothed had also been killed in the fighting.

It was time for Anna to leave the hospital. On the way, Anna was quite animated when describing some of the dishes her mother had taught her to cook. Francesco was practically salivating as he listened. He offered to pick up some groceries for the night's dinner.

They gave him a list for making Chicken Parmesan. By providing the food, he was hoping that he would get an invitation to dinner. Sure enough, Francesco ate with the two ladies. It was every bit gourmet as Anna had described. It occurred to him to ask Josephina if she had money for food with her husband in the hospital and not working. Embarrassed, she was nonetheless honest. He promised he would buy food for them until the ladies could earn enough money to be self-sufficient. Anna beamed.

After he left, Anna said to Josephina, "What a good man he is."

They were in total agreement. He was patient with and kind to all who needed help, and that drew people to him as a leader. His humble way made people love and respect him. Enthusiasm for God and all that was holy was the center of his universe.

It's no wonder that Francesco was attracted to Anna. She was as kind as she was beautiful. She worked for the church making vestments and altar cloths or anything that the priest needed. She cooked for people who were less fortunate. She was gentle and kind when anyone needed something. Her parents had taught her to be unselfish.

Anna resolutely rose before dawn, lit the oil lamps, and ignited the fire in the stove to begin cooking. Josephina went to the well to get water for the pasta. Anna was making meatballs and spaghetti to sell. After they finished their chores of cooking, sewing, and cleaning, they went to the market in Corleone, the *mercantino* (little market). One could sell most anything there. It was a beautiful morning, and lovely colored tarpaulins sheltered the vendors' wares and the ancient medieval streets.

After Anna organized her products, she would shout to entice customers. Her reputation spread regarding her food and her clothing for sale. She made blouses, skirts, pants, dresses, and children's items. Typically, Anna would sell out of whatever she brought for the day and, thus, could contribute well to the Lorenzo household income.

Josephina did laundry for people. She worked tirelessly. Her clientele expanded quickly because of her quality work. Before too long, the two ladies were buying their own groceries without Francesco's help.

Weeks passed, and it was finally time for Bruno to return home. Francesco asked a friend to craft a wheelchair. Anna made some soft cushions for the wheelchair to be comfortable. It was an intense moment for Bruno. They did not know if he would cry or be happy over this new device. It turned out that Bruno was cheerful. He was the type of man who would never pity himself.

Bruno tried to race Francesco home in his wheelchair. Of course, Francesco let him win. At dinner, they explained the happenings since Bruno had been in the hospital. He was ecstatic that Anna was living with them and relieved that the ladies had made so much money. He had fretted over how he would support them. He was determined that he would contribute to the household as well, he just didn't know how yet.

Bruno was a striking man. He had wavy, cocoa-colored hair and always had a twinkle in his brown eyes. When he smiled, his teeth gleamed. He was five feet, ten inches and had a slender, muscular body. The love in his eyes for Josephina was bright and obvious. He would help her with chores, usually joking all the while. It was a pleasure being around him.

While the four new friends talked during dinner, Francesco made an excellent suggestion. He had been thinking of a way to help his invalid friend. When the opportunity presented itself, he asked Bruno to work for him.

"You have two strong arms. That's what it takes to tan leather. I need you to help me with the process of making shoes. Without my father, the business has become so large that I do not have time now to tan the leather for the shoes."

There was a silent pause. Everyone burst out into laughter and then brought out some wine. This was a celebration that the four would remember throughout their lifetimes. Francesco was kind, and he also knew that his new friend would not disappoint him.

CHAPTER 4

BUSINESS

A few days later, Francesco started training Bruno in the art of tanning leather. Francesco began, "There are four stages of tanning leather. The first step is the preparation and cleaning of the hide of an animal. Next, one must pound or thin the skin. The third step is to allow it to rest. The last step is the oiling or polishing of the membrane. Then, it is allowed to cure."

They went through the tanning area and Francesco eagerly showed him examples of each step. Bruno was excited to learn a new trade. There was a large pile of hides obtained from various animals, such as lamb, cow, fox, deer, elk, sheep, and goat.

Next, Francesco showed Bruno the order board, with at least four dozen orders. With the annual *Carnevale* (carnival) scheduled for three weeks from that day, the men both knew they would be working long hours until all the orders were completed and would not be taking the usual siesta time from noon to four o'clock.

Francesco created both practical and luxurious shoes for men, women, and children. If a customer was getting married, he worked on beautiful white leather shoes for the bride and exquisite black leather ones for the groom. Schoolteachers, lawyers, priests, bishops, and friends purchased his fine shoes. With the festival coming, he would produce many striped leather shoes for the women who participated in the parade. The Triolo shop was famous on the island of Sicily for quality workmanship and innovative ideas.

Day after day, new orders came in and products went out. One day, General Roberto Provenza, who had helped Francesco find Josephina, came to see his new boots. He smiled broadly when he saw the shiny, soft boots. He tried them on and paraded around, showing them off.

"Francesco, you have outdone yourself this time!" Francesco was proud and pleased with General Provenza's comment. The general had been in many battles and he continuously had to order new boots.

"Well, sir, I must introduce you to my outstanding tanner." Bruno humbly smiled and nodded to General Provenza.

The general asked him in which battle he had been.

"The most recent mafia battle."

"I was, too. We lost many people," said the general.

Noticing that Bruno did not want to continue the conversation, the gentleman stopped. He walked out with Francesco and told him that the army was planning a surprise attack on the mafia villains.

"We must put an end to these slaughters." After this announcement, the general ducked back in to say, "Thank you, Bruno. I will enjoy my boots."

The next day, a "lady of the night" came in. She had ordered red, sexy shoes with a heel to go with her scant dress. She tried her shoes on and was drunkenly merry. She tripped around the room in her new shoes.

When Francesco told her the price of her shoes, she said, "Wouldn't you rather take it out in trade?"

Both men were embarrassed and pretended not to hear her. She finally gave up on her recruitment efforts and left thanking Francesco, indicating that she would be back.

The men were busily working when three nuns came in to pick up their order. Naturally, the shoes were sturdy, black leather made to last many years. Francesco never charged people of the church.

The next customer presented a creative challenge to Francesco. He was going to be a clown in the festival parade, and he needed a pair of clown shoes. They had to be exaggerated at the toe and much larger than his feet, in white and red leather to match his costume.

"A lovely lady by the name of Anna made my outstanding masquerade, so the shoes need to be outstanding, too."

Francesco looked up from the notes he was taking. "That talented lady is our friend."

"She sure can sew!"

"Thank you," said Francesco. "I will tell her you said so."

When he left, Bruno and Francesco looked at each other and laughed.

"I can't wait to see him in the parade," Bruno said. "I'll bet that we recognize him right away."

An hour later, a filthy street person came in barefooted. His stink even overpowered the tanning chemicals. He wobbled back and forth, weak with hunger. Francesco's eyes traced his long, slender body from his long, tangled, greasy black hair. He looked as though at one time, he had broad muscles over his back and had a thick neck.

"When did you eat last?" inquired Francesco.

"I don't remember," he said.

Francesco had brought fresh vegetables from his garden for lunch with some nice *ciabatta* bread. He asked him to sit down and eat. The homeless man wolfed down the food and drank some water.

"I feel much better now," the bum said.

Straight to the point, Francesco asked him how long he had been a layabout.

"I was in the last mafia battle and I had no idea where my family was because we scattered. We thought that maneuver would help us; instead, it took all of their lives. I don't know what to do now."

It was at that moment that Bruno came out from the back. He had been listening to this man's sad story. The man looked at him. They silently understood each other.

Bruno finally spoke. "I could be wallowing in sorrow for myself, too, but I'm not. Why don't you come home with me and bathe? You can stay at my house tonight. We have an extra blanket and you can sleep on the floor next to the fireplace."

The ragged man could not believe his ears. "You are the first person to offer help to me since the disaster."

" We will continue to work here until Francesco wants to leave. What is your name?"

"Guglielmo," he said.

The shop was busy the rest of the day while the two worked. Bruno was quite exhausted when they decided to close the shop at midnight. He would have stayed there all night, if that had been Francesco's wish. Bruno loved to work with him, because he was so patient and so professional. He knew that his boss had a soft spot in his heart for him, too.

CHAPTER 5

ACCEPTANCE

The women were shocked when Bruno came home with a filthy slacker. Francesco explained his story to the ladies. They immediately put out dinner for the three men. As usual, the food was exceptional, because Anna made it. The stranger ate for an hour. When finished, the ladies showed him where to bathe. Josephina promised new clean clothes that Anna had made.

Early the next morning, Anna made breakfast for five, including Francesco. Clean, starched clothes were offered to the guest. While he was cleaning himself and getting dressed, Francesco spoke to the three.

"I was thinking about offering Guglielmo a job. Bruno and I have been so engaged with the orders, that the shop needs a good cleaning. What do you think, Bruno?"

"I think it's a great idea."

In came Guglielmo for breakfast, somber and well-behaved. His curls were midnight black, and his eyes dark hazel, framed by graceful brows. He certainly looked different from the day before: lean and lithe. His hands were highly calloused.

The five of them enjoyed the food and talked in a relaxed fashion; Anna was curious, so she had to ask the man what job he had before the tragedy.

"I was a supervisor in the sulfur caves. I don't know what shape the mines are in since the skirmish. The owner was killed with his family."

The rest of the conversation was on the lighter side, until Francesco asked Guglielmo if he would like to have a little job cleaning his shop. In addition, Bruno offered him room and board until he had enough money to rent a place. It brought tears to Guglielmo's eyes.

"It's done. Let's leave for work," Francesco said.

As the men walked out into the road, the women looked at each other and were wondering if the other was thinking the same thing. Josephina spoke first.

"I feel so sorry for that man. I was thinking what a hard time I would have with a disabled husband, but there is always someone worse off than you."

"Yes," Anna responded. "He seemed polite and educated. I hope he finds his way."

When the threesome arrived, Guglielmo was ready to start work. Bruno and Francesco were amazed. He did not stop cleaning until the boss said it was lunchtime. Both men shared their fare with him; the ladies had put in extra for him. He sat for only ten minutes and started working with gusto again. By the end of the shift, he had finished the shop halfway; as he went along, he was organizing and labeling everything. The shop had never been so orderly. Francesco was very satisfied.

Around ten o'clock, the men were tired. The two walked with Bruno in his wheelchair to Bruno's house, because Francesco was invited for dinner.

"Did you sell this food at the market today?" Francesco asked Anna.

"Yes, people were lined up in my spot before I got there. I made enough for thirty people, besides our dinner.

I had to turn away some of my customers. The folks that went home empty-handed were not very happy."

Anna also talked about the clothing that she made. She ran out of that, too.

"There is a much bigger demand than I realized."

"Congratulations, Anna," Francesco said.

"I am happy with my success, but I don't know how I am going to keep up with it. I will try to work a longer day."

"Anna, you already work more than twelve hours a day," Francesco said. "It is not healthy for a woman to work more than that." They all concurred.

Then, Bruno spoke up. "Why don't you teach Josephina to sew like you and that might give you more time to make more food."

"That's a good thought," Josephina said.

Anna smiled.

"The highest demand for working men is bib overalls. For casual dress, men want dark jackets that are short, narrow with thin lapels, and rounded in the front. They are buttoned to the top and have short, narrow sleeves that show the shirt cuffs," Anna described. "The dressier pants in most demand are light trousers, narrowed, fitting closely to legs. Shirts are close fitting, also with narrow sleeves and small, stiff collars worn with black bow ties. For dress shirts, men want long, narrow ties.

"The clothing that women want are plain, simple, and practical. For casual wear, the skirts clear the ground for ease of walking. Their shape is a bell form that is snug and smooth over hips with a flared wide hem. What is popular now is to have contrasting fabric such as lace, braids, puffs, frills, gathers, or tucks with pleats and a fancy collar. I make blouses in white, pastels, deep colors, or stripes," Anna said seriously.

"That all sounds complicated," Josephina said.

"You are smart and will learn quickly; we will start tomorrow," Anna said with a smile. "Now, for dessert, I made lemon pie. There is also cream for you to douse on top."

Anna asked Francesco if he was close to finishing his orders for the festival.

"Yes, I think so, if no more come in."

"I am looking forward to *Carnivale*. Will all of you come with me? I love the parade," Anna said. "We will have to work hard to finish the clothing for the dancers in the festival."

Josephina agreed.

"The women have two choices. One is a white silk blouse with a dark blue velvet bodice, which has a mantle; dark blue stockings with long skirts; and Francesco's striped leather shoes, which have ties of black ribbon in the front.

"The second choice has a dimity bodice with red and dark blue or white and dark blue. They have striped skirts and aprons, calfskin slippers with a pointed toe, and dark blue stockings. Kerchiefs wrap around their necks. I hope that last year's jeweler will make the same silver hair clips, filigree drop earrings, rings, and the gorgeous coral necklaces for the participants. They looked stunning!"

Guglielmo asked what she made for the men to wear.

"They will wear dark blue velvet suits, white cotton caps and shirts, a red sash, and two handkerchiefs of red, yellow, or green," Anna said.

"Their second choice is to wear white cotton hose and shirts with wide collars, along with heavy shoes, blue pants, and a wide-brimmed hat made of palm leaves."

"The handkerchiefs will be the easiest to make. Why don't you start teaching me to make them?" Josephina suggested.

Francesco loved to watch Anna get excited. *She is amazing*, he thought.

"We have until two weeks from today for the *feste* (festival or carnival)," said Francesco.

Guglielmo had completely organized the entire shop and put the orders alphabetically, making distribution easy. When completed, he suggested rearranging the shop to make a waiting area and improve their customer service.

"Our timing will be great, just before the rush of the festival. We can put in a large bench for people to sit on, while they are waiting for their order," he explained.

"I like the idea. Bruno, what do you think?"

"I think our customers will keep coming back," he said.

"That's what we want!" Francesco admitted. "Why don't you figure how much the area will cost to build? If it isn't too expensive, we will do it."

That's all Guglielmo needed. He was off in a flash. He negotiated for the supplies, and when Francesco heard the price, he was amazed. In a short time, Francesco and Bruno heard a hammer pounding, with lots of Sicilian songs being sung. Guglielmo was happy for the first time since he lost his family.

He thought he could finish the weekend before the festival. That's when the rush of people would come for their shoes.

Guglielmo also asked Anna if she would teach him how to make cappuccino and espresso for their customers. He was fully invested to help Francesco and Bruno.

The week sped by and people were lined outside the door before opening time. Francesco opened an hour earlier than usual, which was 7 o'clock. The crowd was anxious. Guglielmo had made the coffee at home and kept it heated, so it was nice and hot when people entered the new waiting area. They had each order distributed before lunchtime. People lingered to enjoy their beverage, and on their way out, they raved about the excellent service.

No one ever returned shoes, because Francesco took such care when making them. He even remembered the people who had bunions, callouses, or a crooked toe. His father had taught him well.

CHAPTER 6

MEANT FOR EACH OTHER

The next day was the festival and thoughts rolled around Francesco's head. Guglielmo had left at lunchtime to do an errand. It was then that Francesco approached Bruno. He shuffled his feet a bit bashfully and Bruno knew that his boss wanted to say something. Bruno hoped it wasn't that he no longer needed him. He broke out in a cold sweat. Interestingly, Francesco was sweating, too. He started slowly.

"Bruno, since both Anna's and my parents are deceased, I figured I should talk to you."

Bruno was stumped as to where this conversation might go.

"I want to know if you would bless Anna and me in marriage?"

"Phew!" Bruno began to laugh. Francesco looked confused. Bruno apologized and said that he was not laughing at Francesco. He'd thought Francesco was going to fire him.

Then, Francesco had to laugh. "I would not fire you; you are too valuable. So, will you talk to Josephina and Anna to make sure that everyone approves of our marriage? I would like to propose to Anna tomorrow at the festival."

Bruno agreed wholeheartedly. He said, "You two are meant for each other. I will let you know at dawn tomorrow."

Guglielmo returned and they finished early. Guglielmo asked Francesco if he could speak to him privately. Because Bruno was going home alone that day to speak to the ladies, it would be a fine time for them to talk.

"Do you remember I had said that I worked in the sulfur mines?"

Francesco nodded.

"Do you remember that I told you that the owner and his family were slaughtered?"

"Yes."

"At lunchtime, I went to the records department and spoke to the clerk. I asked him, 'Since the owner was dead and all of his family, too, can someone buy the mines?' His answer was, 'Yes, but only at the auction.'"

"When is the auction?" inquired Francesco.

"Easter Tuesday. What do you think, Francesco? I could run the mines for you, if you buy them. I was the manager before. I know how to recruit the men, what tools we need, and where the best areas are."

Stunned, Francesco replied, "I have never thought of that."

Guglielmo pressed on. "It would be an incredible investment."

"What is involved with sulfur mining?"

"England was our best customer. Sulfur mining is the best contributor to our poor economy, but it's more expensive to run than a farm or ranch. I want you to know, up front, that I completely agree with the teachings of Father Luigi Sturzo. Workers are often mistreated. That will not happen with our men. We will watch carefully if any of the workers contract tuberculosis or any other ailment. Father also expresses the horrible situation of miners forcing children into slave labor. We will have no part in that."

"Hold on a minute, Guglielmo. It's almost like I asked for the time and you told me how the watch was made. I am interested in the *process* of sulfur mining."

"Oh, now I understand," Guglielmo responded.

"Sulfur, an ore, is a yellow powder or crystal. It is not easy to extract. Sulfur is solid at room temperature. So far, we are capturing it through surface strip mining. Powder is put on the top and ignited. It becomes molten and then it is easy to extract.

"Strip mining is almost over, because we do not want to further damage our fertile province. We can work with the local farmers on this. They know how to renew the earth for farming. Once the surface strip mining is exhausted, we will have to dig tunnels with hand tools such as picks. In fact, the tunnels may, in the future, be very deep. Then, the men will put the sulfur in baskets and bring it to the surface. We also use smelting ovens to extract the sulfur.

"The Sicilian way is labor intensive. One of the miners said he thought it was so hot in the tunnels, he felt like he was in hell. That is why I will need to hire experienced men to do this part of the mining process. Once we tunnel underground, we will use the American process, called the Frasch Method. We can place tubes or hoses in the tunnel and pump hot water into the deposits. This will melt the sulfur, which will solidify. This system produces the highest purity. Do you want to hear something funny?"

"Yes," Francesco said, dazed by the detail.

Guglielmo continued, "You know the wax in our ears? It's partly sulfur!"

"What a lesson I have had today!" Francesco said, laughing. "Tomorrow I am going to propose marriage to Anna Monteleone. Bruno is talking to the ladies now, to seek their approval. If Anna agrees to marry me and she likes your proposition, I will go to the auction and see what happens."

"That is all I can ask for," Guglielmo said.

"Do we have to sign up?"

"Yes, I have the paperwork. We need to submit it before Easter Sunday."

Francesco traveled home alone. He couldn't wait until the next morning. Bruno would tell him if Anna agreed. Dinner was not appealing to him because Anna had not made it and he did not like his own cooking. A restless night ensued. All he could think about was Anna's answer. He got up several times, hoping that it was dawn. It wasn't. He thought of different ways to ask Anna to be his wife. He had the bright idea to propose when the fireworks were exploding. Anna loved the show. That could make the perfect memory.

Dawn finally came, and he was already cleaned up and wearing the nice shirt that Anna had made him. He paced back and forth, looking out the window for Bruno. It seemed like days had passed. Finally, Bruno was at his door, with a smile on his face.

"What did Anna say?" he asked.

"Well, she said, oh, I forgot," Bruno said mercilessly.

Francesco stopped pacing.

Bruno started to laugh and belted out Anna's answer, in a high voice: "Yes, I don't want to be with any other man but Francesco!"

He danced with glee around the room in an awkward, manly, sort of way.

He garbled out, "When can I go see her?"

"The ladies and Guglielmo are ready to leave for the festival, so anytime that you are ready."

"I'm ready!" Francesco said in a singsong voice. "Let's leave now."

They were out the door in no time. Francesco ran and jumped like a scalawag down the road. They arrived shortly. Francesco had a wide grin. Anna returned the look. It was going to be a wonderful day.

They found a space where they could see the parade. After this day, Lent would start, so Anna had made some delicacies that wouldn't be eaten again for forty days, such as glazed orange rinds, nuts, and candies. No one hesitated to start.

For lunch, she had prepared *antipasti* with different salamis, hams, peppers, cheeses, pickled pig's feet, pasta with sardines, and garlic bread. In addition, they had chicken and hard-cooked eggs. They ate lunch at eleven o'clock because no one could wait.

The parade was going by that time. Men and women danced in Anna's costumes and Francesco's shoes. The clown acknowledged Anna and Francesco, showing off his hilarious shoes and outfit. Children sang traditional Sicilian songs. Instruments such as tambourines, horns, accordions, violins, harmonicas, and flutes accompanied the singers and dancers.

The parade concluded in the *chiazza* (city square), where there were arts, crafts, games, and shows. When people saw Anna, they asked why she didn't have a food or clothing exhibit. She had spent so much time on making costumes, that there was no more time. Francesco was asked why he had no shoe display. Bruno and Guglielmo were asked about shoes and tanning. Others asked Josephina to do their laundry. It seemed that they were known by all of the Corleone population.

Before they knew it, dinnertime came. They indulged in refreshments such as wine, pasta puttanesca, bread, seafood, and various meats and cheeses. It was nearly six o'clock and the fireworks were about to begin. Bruno winked at Francesco. Josephina, Guglielmo, and he made an excuse to wander in a different direction.

When Anna and Francesco found the perfect spot to view the fireworks, he started. "The first time I ever saw your face, when you were mired in blood, on the battlefield, I knew that you would become my wife and the mother of my children."

Anna's eyes widened and she covered her smile as she tried not to laugh.

He continued, "Would you marry me, my love?"

Next came three explosions. One with the fireworks, one with Francesco kissing Anna, and one when she responded with a "Yes."

Francesco slipped the promise ring on her finger.

She had fallen in love watching him care for Bruno, Josephina, Guglielmo, and herself.

"You are a man with great compassion and kindness. You are my pillar of tenderness, caring, and warmth. I want to spend the rest of my life with you and have your beautiful children."

"You are my pillar of endearment," Francesco said back to her.

"When would you like to be married?"

She had thought about it all day.

"June, when the *Carretto Siciliano* (Sicilian Carriage Festival) begins. If you don't mind, I would like a small, quiet ceremony with Bruno, Josephina, and Guglielmo. June marks the one-year anniversary of the death of our parents."

Francesco thought what she suggested was very appropriate. Francesco and Anna kissed passionately with tears of joy in their eyes.

Shortly afterward, the gang returned to the couple. Francesco announced that the wedding would be in June. Bruno whistled loudly, Josephina hugged Anna, and Guglielmo shook Francesco's hand. They talked all the way home, joyously.

CHAPTER 7

DILIGENCE

N ews came that General Roberto Provenza and his men had arrested some Sicilian mobsters. When the general and his men went to town announcing the news, there was cheering and dancing. Once more, the Sicilians could feel free.

When the soldiers reached Corleone, General Provenza made a special stop at the cobbler shop to tell the men about their victory. Bruno whistled loudly. Francesco shook the general's hand.

The general continued. "When we were in battle, I thought of you, Bruno, and everyone else who was injured or killed." Bruno sincerely thanked him with a shaky, emotional voice.

That night at dinner, Francesco, Bruno, and Guglielmo discussed what a fine job General Provenza had done. The mayor called for a holiday. Francesco and Anna used the time to plan their wedding. The two ladies and men leisurely walked to *Santa Rosalia* church. The priest had finished all the morning Masses and welcomed the loving couple. Father Primo knew Anna because she made all of the vestments for the church and because she and the others attended Mass there every Sunday.

Francesco began, "Father Primo, will you marry us?"

"Yes, of course. When do you want the ceremony?"

"In June, if that is possible, during the Carriage Festival Week." They watched Father Primo write it on his calendar for two o'clock.

"Thank you, Father," they said in unison.

As they walked, Josephina jokingly asked Anna if she was sure she wanted to get married."

When they got home and settled, Francesco explained to his future bride about the sulfur mines and the auction. He asked her if she thought it was a good idea. Knowing the value of sulfur, coupled with how responsible Guglielmo was, she said "Yes," with no hesitation.

"Then I will go to the auction with Guglielmo and Bruno."

Easter finally came. The Roman Catholics refer to Jesus as the "lamb of God"; thus, lamb was a traditional Easter meal. Anna asked the group what they would like to accompany the lamb.

"Fresh fruits and vegetables with garlic bread," said Bruno. Francesco wanted raviolis and meatballs.

They had been fasting for the forty days of Lent and were ready to eat everything, faster than they could make it.

Anna and Josephina made the raviolis. The first filling consisted of freshly grated Romano cheese, chopped spinach, breadcrumbs, eggs, ground beef, ground pork, onions, garlic, and spices. The second filling was made of fresh, homemade, grated mozzarella, homemade ricotta cheese, eggs, grated Romano cheese, onions, garlic, and seasonings.

Sicilians have many traditions. Upon adding the last ingredient to a recipe, the ladies make the sign of the cross and pronounce that it is dedicated to the Pope.

They rolled out the dough as long as the kitchen table. This was the first dough. When finished, it was draped over several continuous broomstick handles, suspended horizontally by special ceiling hooks that Francesco had installed. The hooks were removable when not in use. The delicate dough was covered with dampened towels, so it stayed fresh and soft. It would become the top of the raviolis.

The second dough was covered with the filling. The first dough was then placed on top. They then pressed a small cup into the dough to form the cheese raviolis, cut along the cup indentations and produced the delicate pillows. Anna pinched the edge of dough with a fork, so the filling would not leak out when boiled. The process with the meat filling was identical.

They needed to rest after their tedious work. Out in the vegetable garden, they relaxed with cool lemonade. The men were tending the garden and the orchard. Tradition dictated that the men would say, "Whatever I eat today, may I eat it next year." Figs were dried in a basket and not touched until the feast day of St. Francis of Assisi, October 4. The moths would ruin them unless they were protected by the saint.

After their short respite, the task of making mounds of meatballs with ground beef and pork, milk, bread, eggs, onions, cheese, and seasonings were completed in a flash by their experienced hands. They began singing ancient Sicilian songs. The men picked the fresh vegetables and fruit in the garden and joined in the singing.

~ ~ ~

The next day, Easter Monday, was a holiday. Bruno and Guglielmo met with Francesco to discuss the purchase of the sulfur mines. Guglielmo explained the procedures of the auction. He talked about the worth of the land and the potential of sulfur. Francesco had to set the highest price he would pay. Fortunately, he and his family had saved money for an opportunity like this.

The auction began at nine o'clock in the morning, so the men were there at eight-thirty. The mines were number twenty-four, the last item on the list to be sold. As the day wore on, Francesco noticed that the mayor had joined the crowd. He tipped his hat to the mayor and the mayor acknowledged Francesco in return.

The auctioneers were ready for the sale of the mines. Someone made the first bid, and then a second, third, and fourth bid was made in rapid succession. Francesco got nervous. Guglielmo nudged Francesco.

Then, most people dropped out because the bid was so high. One bidder continued. Back and forth, back and forth, the bids were made. Bruno noticed that the mayor made a signal to Francesco's competitor. The man suddenly stopped bidding and Francesco was the owner of the mines. It had happened so quickly that Francesco made another bid that he didn't need to make. People laughed, and the auctioneer did not hold him responsible for his last bid.

Francesco went to sign official papers. The three couldn't wait to tell the ladies. While walking to Bruno's, Bruno asked Francesco and Guglielmo if either one had noticed the mayor's signal. Neither had.

When the ladies heard the news, Anna hugged Francesco and then pulled back because that was not appropriate unless they were married. But Francesco didn't mind a bit.

During dinner, Guglielmo answered everyone's questions. He still had his hand tools, but Francesco needed other machines and could save a lot of money if he purchased them at the auctioneer's office.

The next day, the men went to the mines. Bruno's wheelchair did not fit so he waited outside. Francesco was a quick learner and Guglielmo was a good teacher.

The first thing to do was to hire men for the job. All three men could read and write, but most people couldn't. Guglielmo drew pictures announcing the jobs at the mines. The flyers were distributed all over Corleone. Men were expected to show up for interviews in a week. Most of the men who had worked under Guglielmo wanted their old job back. Everyone who showed up was a good worker, except Digger. Digger not only dug for sulfur but also dug into people's personal affairs looking to blackmail them. Guglielmo warned Francesco about him.

Digger arrived agitated and drunk. He insisted that he be hired as a manager. Francesco explained that they did not need another manager besides Guglielmo. Digger shouted, *"Va al diavolo!"* ("Go to the devil!") and caused quite a scene.

Italians often use hand gestures to express themselves. One of the workers who disliked Digger gave him a chin flick with the back of his hand, which means, "Who cares?" Another miner placed his right index finger near the temple of the brain, and made circular motions, symbolizing that Digger was crazy.

At those men, Digger pushed his right arm up in the air forming an "L"; he took his left hand and hit the inside of his right elbow. This movement and saying "*Vaffanculo,*" (the F-word equivalent) was the worst of all.

Guglielmo and Francesco stood tall, with their arms folded across their chests. Digger grabbed for Guglielmo's shirt and attempted to swing at him, but he fell to the ground instead. Even in his drunken stupor, he knew he should leave. Everyone laughed as he stumbled away, yelling more profanities and threatening Francesco and Guglielmo. Next, he took his right index finger, pointed to Francesco and Guglielmo and drew circles in the air. It meant, "see you later." Digger would get his revenge another time.

This fiasco made Francesco realize that he needed to go to the mines daily with Guglielmo and share his time with Bruno at the shoe shop.

Both businesses went well. Francesco was exhausted but persisted. He wanted to be able to buy anything Anna wanted when they got married. There was not much that Anna requested. She spent only what she needed for her business and little on herself. Josephina was improving as a seamstress, and thus, Anna now could make food for fifty people.

One bright and beautiful day, lines had already formed when the ladies arrived at the *mercantino*. It was peaceful enough until they got closer to selling out of the food. One man started a ruckus shoving his way to the front of the line. But a large man at the front, who stood well over six feet tall and was muscular like a fighter, would not tolerate someone getting in front of him.

One swing put the intruder on the ground, but he got up clenching his fists. Other men joined into the brawl. It was a disaster.

"Someone call the police," a customer shouted. It took quite a while before peace was restored. After hearing Anna out, the police allowed people not involved in the fight a place in line. The rest were locked up in jail.

During dinner that night, the two ladies shared the story. They were truly upset. Anna thought that she should move her tent closer to the police station and hire another lady. The helper could serve food while Anna was the cashier. Francesco gave his blessing to the plan. Guglielmo drew pictures advertising for the job which were distributed around Corleone.

A dozen or so women interviewed. Most of them were not up to Anna's standards of how to use certain spices or how long to cook certain dishes. One stood out. She could answer all of Anna's questions correctly. The new employee was invited to dinner to meet everyone.

At first glance, Francesco said, "I know you. You are the lady who wears a tiny size three shoe!"

She blushed. Anna introduced her as Maria Margherita. She felt welcomed.

Maria lived with her parents, a brother and two sisters on the north side of town. Her parents needed her to work to increase the family income, because she was the oldest. Maria felt like she belonged in the kitchen with Anna.

"This is the best possible job for me. My prayers are answered," Maria said.

Anna was touched by Maria's openness and enthusiasm. Maria seemed a little alarmed at the previous day's brawling, but Anna set her mind at ease by telling her the police came to her rescue.

"You know, it's a good thing that the chief of police loves my food. He said he did not want anything to interfere with it. I deliver food to his house twice a week."

"It's important to know people in high places!" Maria said, laughing. "Have you ever asked the mayor if he wanted meals delivered to him?"

"No, but Francesco has a relationship with him, and I will ask him to talk to the mayor."

CHAPTER 8

NO GREATER LOVE

One night around dinner, the five friends talked about the wedding. "I am glad that Francesco agreed to a simple, small wedding. All that tradition would be wonderful, but it wouldn't be right without our parents."

They had many choices of Catholic churches for the wedding that reflected Sicilian occupational history. A bride could choose a Norman, Arabian, Romanesque, Gothic, or other architectural style. Anna chose her neighborhood church, the Sanctuary of *Santa Rosalia*, a Baroque church.

This church was unusual because it was built connected to a dark, gloomy cave. People believed that *Santa Rosalia* had lived in the cave. When you walk in, water drips on your head. It is a wonder, walking through the opulent part of the church to the left, with a dismal cave connected to it on the right. The church is on top of *Monte Pellegrino* (Pilgrim's Mountain), which overlooks the whole bay of Palermo. *Santa Rosalia* is special, because she cured a plague miraculously in Palermo. The people around Palermo refer to her affectionately as *"La Santuzza"* ("the cute little saint").

Francesco shared with Maria that he and Anna were to be married in June. Without hesitation, she said that she would cook, so Anna would enjoy her wedding day.

"I will make suits for all three men," said Josephina.

"Would it be okay if I requested that you make a dress for me?" Maria asked.

"Of course. We will all look beautiful," Josephina said.

The wedding day was fast approaching. Anna tried on her gown in a closed room. The dress was modest but beautiful. It was white cotton with a natural waistline and had a portrait neckline rounding her lovely shoulders. She preferred long sleeves and a closed back. Josephina only had to take a few nips and tucks to make it fit. Anna tried on her shoes with the gown and they went perfectly together.

After 1840, brides wore white dresses, because Britain's Queen Victoria set the trend when she married Prince Albert. In 1858, Mendelssohn's "Wedding March" was played for the wedding of her daughter, Princess Victoria, and it became a tradition in many cultures, including Sicily.

Josephina began to cry. "I wish your parents were here to see how beautiful their daughter looks."

Anna turned with tears in her eyes and said, "Me, too!"

"In addition to your gown, I made you a new mattress for your wedding gift. I found enough cornstalks to make it firm. Bruno enjoys a firm mattress, so I thought Francesco would, too."

"Thank you so much! I had not thought of that, because I have been so busy," said Anna. "I cannot wait to tell Francesco—or maybe you and Bruno should tell him."

Each man tried on his suit and Josephina tailored them to their size and shape. Maria also came by to have her dress fitted. Lastly, Anna tailored Josephina's dress because it was too difficult for her to tailor her own.

The next day came and Father Primo was waiting for them at *Santa Rosalia*. They'd rehearsed their vows many times in preparation for their marriage Mass.

"My Dearest Anna,

The first time we met, I fell deeply in love with you even though we were young. I knew that you were the one with whom I wanted to spend the rest of my life. Every moment we have spent together since that day, my love for you has grown. I love you with all that I am, all that I have been, and all that I will ever be, with all of my heart. You are the most amazing and perfect woman I have ever known! You make me happier than I ever thought possible. I am truly blessed that you have agreed to be my wife. Today, I make the sincerest promise one heart can make to another. I vow to be your forever love and support, your devoted partner in life. From this day forward, I will love and console you, hold you close, and remain faithful to you all the days of our lives. I offer this in love and joy," said Francesco solemnly.

Then, Anna began, "My Beloved Francesco,

From the moment that we met, to this moment, looking into your eyes, I see you now not only as a man but as a father, too. I have always loved you, even before we met. I promise to embrace every stage that our future holds. My first love, my only love, you're every breath that I take and heartbeat that I have, my best friend and the man of my dreams. There can be no greater love than what I feel for you. No words can express how much I love you, not only because you are the love of my life, but my hero, too.

Today, I give you my mind, my hand, my heart, and my love without condition, completely and forever. Today, tomorrow, and for the rest of my days, I promise to stand beside you, to dance with you in times of joy, to console you in times of sadness, to rejoice with you in times of health, and to soothe you in times of illness. I promise to turn to you for happiness, solace, encouragement, and for inspiration. I am a better person when I am with you. I promise to be faithful and true to you with love and affection, every happy, sad, and blessed day, for the rest of our lives."

They kissed, and their four friends clapped. Father Guido Primo congratulated the blissful couple; he remarked that he had never witnessed a more devoted, beautiful, and loving bride and groom.

Bruno waited to go outside to let out a whistle of joy.

The wedding feast featured ricotta gnocchi with pesto sauce, linguini and clams, roasted vegetables, and a corn and avocado salad. Then came the *torrone* (nougat-based candy with honey, egg whites, flavorings, and nuts), which had been invented in Cremora, Italy, for aristocratic weddings. Wine flowed freely. *"Buon vinu fa sangu!"* ("Good wine makes good blood!")

They all joked and laughed about silly little things. When the decorated *cassata* (cake) came out, everyone had forks ready.

Soon, it was late and time for Anna and Francesco to begin their married life. They all called the traditional wedding salutation, *"Per cent'anni!"* ("For a hundred years!")

Bruno and Josephina left with them as surrogate parents. They made the wedding bed and tossed coins in the sheets for good fortune. Then they hugged and kissed the newlyweds and parted company.

Meanwhile, Maria and Guglielmo stayed behind, as earlier they had agreed to clean the dishes and kitchen. Guglielmo studied Maria while working.

"When we are done cleaning, can we sit and talk?" Guglielmo asked.

Maria agreed.

CHAPTER 9

DIGNITY

When Bruno and Josephina returned to their home, they opened a bottle of wine and sat down with Guglielmo and Maria.

"Maria, tell us more about yourself and your family," Guglielmo probed.

Maria felt awkward talking so seriously to a man; she had never done that.

Maria began with a quivering voice, "As you know, my parents, Luciano and Sebastiana are living, and I have one brother and two sisters." She cleared her throat. "My parents need me to work because they are having financial difficulty."

She looked at the group; she could tell they deeply understood. They stayed silent to let her continue.

"The truth is, my father drinks too much and cannot keep a steady job. My mother does not discuss it in front of the children, because he gets furious, and she doesn't want them to know. They are young enough for her to hide his secret."

"I have a suggestion," Guglielmo said. "Would you like me to invite your father to work in the sulfur mines with me?"

"That would be wonderful," Maria said.

"Is your brother old enough to work there, too?"

"Yes, and he would be a hard worker," Maria said.

"Fine. When do you want me to speak with them?"

"Is it possible for you to come to my house tomorrow? My parents are awake by seven in the morning."

"I surely will," Guglielmo said.

Maria was so anxious to share the plan that she skipped all the way home.

The next thing that Maria knew, Guglielmo was knocking on the door. The family was excited to accept his offer. He knew that Francesco would be happy about it; however, he told them that he had to speak with his boss for final approval. They expected that.

"I will let you know Wednesday at this time. Francesco and his new bride are on their honeymoon right now. Before I leave, I must tell you what a hard-working daughter you have and what a sensational cook she is. The wedding meal she prepared was amazing."

Mr. Margherita agreed with him. "She has learned a lot from Anna. I hope we get to meet your friends soon. Maria has said remarkable things about them."

"You will meet them soon, Mr. Ghiselli. I will make sure of that."

"With the sharing of good news, may I ask you to chaperone Maria and me tonight for a walk?"

They had suspected that Maria might be interested in someone.

"No," Luciano responded. "She needs to stay with her family."

Guglielmo was shocked and unhappy. He left feeling awkward. Francesco and Anna would arrive home late the next day, so he would discuss hiring Maria's father and brother then.

Guglielmo left to find a place of his own and found one close to where Maria lived. He was making enough money to be self-sufficient now. At dinnertime, it seemed odd with just the three of them eating together.

Francesco and Anna honeymooned in Taormina, on the east side of the island and the hub of the *Carretto Siciliano* festival. When they arrived home, they had some traditions that needed to be addressed. Newlyweds believed that moving into a first home needed to be accompanied by a ritual to rid the house of any spirits that could harm the new couple or their first child. In the Triolos' case, they had invited Father Primo to bless or exorcise their home. Father Primo was just leaving when Guglielmo arrived.

As was the custom, Guglielmo brought three gifts: a broom, salt, and a hard-cooked egg. A broom symbolized that they would always have a clean home. Salt was a token gift that represented good health for the couple and their family. The egg represented fertility. Francesco and Anna were grateful for such thoughtful gifts.

Anna swept the floor, paying close attention to the corners. If the floor was swept properly and had no spiders, the home would not have any evil spirits in it.

Asking about their honeymoon was a polite way to begin talking. They had never seen carriages that compared to the magnificent ones they saw at the festival. The vibrant reds, yellows, greens, and blues stood out in many different designs on the wheels and carriages themselves. Panels on the sides of the wagons depicted Sicilian kings and noblemen, battles that had been fought and won, famous Sicilian castles, the Palermo Cathedral, piazzas, and many other themes. Images of medieval times were often in Sicilian minds. An abundance of dyed plumes and gold regalia were just some of the details on the carriages. Remarkable Arabian horses from Trieste were specially picked at an early age to be trained to pull the carriages; they held their heads and tails high. When music played at the festival, it was high spirited, and the horses' amazing prancing was in step with the beat.

"It was quite a spectacle to see," Anna shared excitedly. The Lipizzan horse, a kind of Arabian, has a high step and energetic gait. They arch their necks and hold their weight on their hind legs and can hop with their forelegs under their body. They can also kick out their back legs and jump simultaneously. They are sturdy, fast, beautiful, and intelligent. Young horses are gray, but the adults turn white.

Naturally, a honeymoon for four days was not enough time, but they had responsibilities at home. They inquired about how things went in their absence. Guglielmo recounted the events. He said he had conditionally hired Luciano Margherita and his son, pending Francesco's approval.

"Of course." Only one thing surprised him; Maria's father had refused to chaperone Guglielmo's walk with her.

"Perhaps, if you two, Bruno and Josephina met the father and the rest of Maria's family, Mr. Margherita would know that I have the best of intentions," Guglielmo said.

"Why don't you ask Maria and her family for supper next Sunday after Mass?" Anna said. "Bruno and Josephina will come, as well."

Guglielmo could not wait for Maria's father and brother to start working with him. They all showed up at the mines early in the morning. The father seemed like he was in a much better mood. Guglielmo explained the responsibilities related to the job; then, he asked his most skilled man to train them the next couple of days. They both were quick studies.

When closing time came on the second day, Guglielmo extended the invitation for Sunday's meal. He reminded Luciano that he had expressed interest in meeting the two couples. Surprisingly, Mr. Margherita accepted. After he departed, Guglielmo merrily ran to Francesco at the shoe shop. Both Francesco and Bruno were happy for him.

"We will have a great time," Francesco said.

When Anna heard the news, she started to make her "gravy" (tomato sauce) that evening. Francesco suggested making lasagna and meatballs.

In addition, she planned to make *Chicken Saltimbocco* (means jump in your mouth), calamari stuffed with shrimp, and her luscious *focaccia* bread. For dessert, she liked to make *tiramisu* (lady fingers, espresso, sugar, and cream).

Sunday arrived, and Guglielmo was a wreck. He was so nervous that he forgot to buy flowers for Sebastiana, Maria's mother. He bolted to the flower purveyor; luckily, someone had ordered roses but did not pick them up.

Francesco was out chopping wood and Bruno was helping him stack it when Guglielmo arrived. Within ten minutes, the Margherita family came. When Guglielmo presented the flowers to Sebastiana Margherita, she blushed and had a smile as wide as the sea.

Luciano appeared to be in good spirits. Josephina had made *antipasti* for everyone. They were eaten in no time, but the conversation was lively, so no one noticed. Maria's papa had a lot of questions. He was quite impressed with the story of how everyone met.

"Had it not been for Francesco bringing me to the hospital," Anna related, "the doctor said I could have bled to death."

Francesco humbly accepted the credit.

Maria observed her father and noticed that his face had softened. A new respect had developed toward Guglielmo as a caring boss.

Josephina added that Francesco had accompanied her to the hospital every day for many weeks to visit Bruno.

Supper was ready and cards on the table designated who sat where. Maria's younger brother and sisters raced to the table. They held up their knife and fork vertically, eager. Francesco included a special prayer for the Margheritas and how he hoped that they all would become the best of friends. Maria's father added a thanksgiving prayer that they had the opportunity to meet.

The food and wine were delightful; they were too busy eating and drinking to talk much. At last, their attention turned to the dessert and Anna gracefully served everyone; then, a second helping. Laughing, Anna, Josephina, and Maria romped around the table to satisfy all the requests for more cake.

When leaving, the Margheritas gave the traditional Italian hug, a double hug. One hug is for the left side of the face and the next for the right side of the face. If they had known each other better, they would have kissed each side of the cheek.

The original five stayed. They felt fairly confident that Luciano enjoyed their company, and they clearly knew that Sebastiana, had a marvelous time. She had mentioned they don't get out much. Guglielmo was hopeful.

CHAPTER 10

PATIENCE

Even though Luciano was a hard worker, Guglielmo learned that he had unpredictable moods. He was quick-tempered, nasty, and repugnant to his son on one day; then, the next day, he would be pleasant, friendly, and agreeable. On his "touchy" days, he was unapproachable. Maria told Guglielmo that her poor mother had to ignore and endure his moods, or there would be a terrible argument in front of the children.

"When would be a good time for me to approach him again on the subject of courting?"

Maria was stumped. "I think we have to see what mood he is in before you talk to him," she said. "Unfortunately, my father sees me as a "paycheck." That's why he doesn't want me to get involved with a man. Maybe if he is in a good mood, my brother tells you, and that might be the time you address him."

"Okay, tell your brother our plan."

Days later, Maria excused herself from their *mercantino* space after it had quieted down. Anna was surprised. Maria had never done that before. She was talking to a man that Anna had never seen. He was making her cry. He had a curiously wry smile on his face.

When Maria returned, she was wiping the tears from her eyes. Anna was alarmed. "Who was that man, Maria, and what did he say to you?"

Maria sloughed it off. There was a silence between them, but luckily, more customers had come to buy food. Anna had never seen Maria so sad.

When the day was over and the ladies were cleaning up, Anna again asked Maria if she could help her. A very troubled look was her only response. It was as though Maria was looking past Anna. They walked home silently. Usually, Maria walked to Anna's house with her, but not that day.

Francesco came home that evening to find Anna weeping. She described the events of the day.

"Can you describe the man for me, so I can share the information with Guglielmo?"

"He was about five feet, nine inches, with thick, jet-black hair and a mustache. His skin is fair, and he has a distinct scar on his left cheek resembling the letter "Y." He is thin and had an arrogant, wicked look on his face. He frightened me."

As soon as Anna referred to the scar on his face, Francesco knew, Digger. "After supper, I will go to Guglielmo's place to warn him."

"Before you go, Guglielmo needs to know that Maria did not want to acknowledge it. I asked her twice if I could help her. I could tell that she was afraid, but she refused to discuss it. Could it be about her father's debt?"

"I will ask Guglielmo if Digger is a shylock. He would know."

Francesco brought in the necessary water from the well to help Anna.

"You are my pillar of strength, Francesco."

Anna began cleaning the dishes. She readied all the pots that she and Maria would need the next morning. She chopped the fresh tomatoes, carrots, celery, and onion for the *sofrito*. She wanted the dough of the sunflower-seed bread to be perfect, so that it would have plenty of time to rise. During her baking, Anna spilled salt, so as tradition required, she took a pinch of salt and threw it over her left and right shoulders to ward off bad luck. If she spilled olive oil, it was expected that she put a dab of olive oil behind her ears for the same reason.

Great effort went into the creation of bread. Bread recipes were cherished and shared from generation to generation. Before the bread was baked, Anna made the sign of the cross over it, praying that it would be perfect.

Bread symbolized the body of Christ. During Mass, unleavened bread is transformed symbolically into Christ's body by the priest. No matter how stale bread might get, one could never throw it away, unless it was kissed first, which showed respect to Jesus. They had to ensure that bread never fell upside down because it scorned Christ.

Francesco returned from Guglielmo's.

"What was Guglielmo's reaction to Maria's visitor?" she asked Francesco, "And how is he going to handle Maria not wanting to discuss it?"

"Guglielmo was not surprised," Francesco said. "Digger gives loans with impossible deadlines. But people who are in debt are desperate. The Margheritas now have three people working, so their situation should be improving. As for Guglielmo respecting Maria's wishes on this subject, I don't know how to advise him."

"Maybe Maria will share something with Guglielmo, so he doesn't have to ask," Anna said, doubtfully. "It's getting late, Francesco. Are you ready for bed?"

He was ready—and wanting to frolic. Anna loved it when he was in that mood. They always enjoyed each other rapturously. They were a little too exuberant that night; the bed broke. They tried to repair the framework in the early hours of the morning. Just when they were finishing, Maria knocked on the door. Anna asked her to start cooking while she got dressed.

When Anna entered the kitchen, Maria had a despondent look on her face. It would be a long day. Maria said barely a word, but Anna tried to talk as she normally would.

Weeks passed. Digger came regularly to speak with Maria. Each time he did, Maria seemed a little more desperate and a lot more depressed. Two things were occurring simultaneously: Maria spoke less and less, and every time Guglielmo asked her brother if Mr. Margherita was in a good mood, the brother said, "No." Maria told Guglielmo to stop asking.

Finally, Guglielmo approached Francesco about it. "Maria and I agreed that her brother would tell me when the papa was in a good mood, so I could ask her father if he would chaperone us on a walk? Now Maria is avoiding me and telling me not to ask anymore. What do you think is happening?"

Francesco was a kind man, but he thought he should tell Guglielmo exactly what he was thinking. "I am not happy about what I am going to say, Guglielmo, but I don't think Maria is ready for a relationship with you.

Perhaps you should give up on the idea and court someone else."

Guglielmo had tears in his eyes. "I am so lonesome, but I agree with you, as much as I hate to admit it." He sighed, and his shoulders slumped. Resigned, he continued, "One of my miner friends has a sister, Mirella, who is interested in me. She brings lunch every day for my friend, and once in a while, she brings me lunch, too."

"You are being wise to pursue someone else," Francesco sadly commented. "When I get home tonight, I will explain all of this to Anna."

Anna was distressed when Francesco described the agreement.

"They would have made such a beautiful couple," she said, resolving to try and ignore Maria's meetings with Digger, to respect her friend's silence, even though it would be difficult.

CHAPTER 11

GRACIOUSNESS

Some Sicilian food is savory and flavorful and it reflects the influence of a diverse cultural inheritance. Inspiration from the Arabs is particularly noticeable. The food may even be hot and spicy, such as *pasta con le sarde* (pasta, sardines, raisins, pine nuts, and capers), *frittedda* (peas, fava beans, and artichokes), and *pasta con la melanzane* (pasta with eggplant). Anna had a repertoire.

Anna and Maria were in the kitchen at three o'clock in the morning on May 1. The mayor wanted garlic bread and this was the perfect day to make it. On May 1, ladies must make bread to have good luck in their family until the next May. The legend behind the belief tells of a woman who denied crumbs from her bread to a beggar and was generous to devils, masquerading as knights. She was punished for her actions.

They were hoping that donkeys, "Lazy" and "Loafer," would cooperate that morning. When customers could not pay Anna, they offered chickens or a turkey or something else. Both donkeys had been payment.

They went to Niccollo's, the mayor's house, to introduce themselves. The mayor was delighted when Anna told him that they had cooked tripe with tomato sauce, macaroni, roasted vegetables, and garlic bread. She knew that was his favorite and his first choice.

As they arrived, the mayor was licking his lips and rubbing his hands together.

"Dinnertime cannot come fast enough today," he said. "I will be thinking about the food all day."

"Wonderful," Anna replied. "We will bring another meal in two days."

"Thank you most graciously," Niccollo said.

Soon after, the ladies made it to their space at the market. A crowd was already waiting.

The mayor stopped into Francesco's shoe shop the next day. He marveled at the new bench addition and the offering of espresso. "I dropped in to tell you that Anna's dinner was delicious! It was just like my mother's cooking, God rest her soul. I assure you that is a highly deserved compliment."

"Great!" Francesco responded. "They will return tomorrow."

"I will be waiting anxiously for them!"

The two ladies were in the kitchen bright and early on Friday, when the mayor was expecting another meal. They were making butternut squash raviolis with a feather-like dough. The tomatoes were simmering and the red bell peppers were roasting. The delicious scent of fresh-baked bread was in the air.

"Maria, your idea to cook for the mayor worked out well. Niccollo spoke to other dignitaries and before I knew it, there were five other important people ordering food from us. Anna was happy because her regular customers had been slowly dwindling. Times were getting extremely difficult and the economy weakened more each month. Many people could no longer afford to buy prepared food. The clothing business had been diminishing, as well."

When they arrived, they told the mayor what they had cooked.

"Fantastic! Enough with the free food! I want to pay and schedule you for three times a week. Is that possible?"

"We would be happy to accommodate that schedule for you."

At dinner, Anna summarized her conversation with the mayor.

"He paid us twice as much as we had requested. But it may have been for the two meals," Anna added.

"Let's wait and see," Francesco said. He would not be surprised if the mayor did pay twice the amount they had quoted him. Later they discovered Francesco was right.

Monday was the next day for food delivery, giving them two days to prepare. The ladies started cooking their delicacies. After a while, they were fatigued, so they sat at the dinner table.

Coincidentally on purpose, Guglielmo sat by Maria, who listened to the conversations attentively. She looked at these wonderful people with great admiration.

CHAPTER 12

TRUST

The following week, Guglielmo arranged to meet Bernardo, the miner, and his father, Onofrio Caparelli. Guglielmo asked Onofrio if he would chaperone a walk with Mirella, his daughter, and himself. Onofrio and his wife, Luriline, were pleased that Guglielmo had asked. Their first walk was scheduled for the coming Friday after work.

Mirella's parents made dinner for Guglielmo. It was a pleasant evening, but he could not get Maria out of his mind. He reasoned with himself that Maria was impossible to pursue, so he tried not to be nonresponsive when he was with Mirella. It didn't work. Mirella sensed something was wrong, and she asked him about it. Of course, Guglielmo denied it, but Mirella knew differently.

After several weeks of chaperoned walks, Anna asked Guglielmo if he would like to invite Mirella and her family to dinner so they could meet. He responded favorably, but it was obvious that he was ambivalent. They determined that Sunday after Mass would be a good time.

Sunday came, and after Mass, Guglielmo went to Francesco's home early to help chop the wood for cooking, set up the big table, pick fruits and vegetables, and do whatever else he could to help. Mirella shared that her father's favorite meal was pasta with shrimp scampi. Anna loved that dish, too.

Onofrio, Luriline, and Mirella arrived. This time Guglielmo had remembered flowers for Luriline. As always, dinner was exquisite, and the Caparellis could not say enough good things about it.

The dessert was next. When the cannolis came out, Onofrio smiled a wide grin. Anna had made them with mascarpone cheese, ricotta, rose water, chocolate pieces, and glazed oranges. The filling was extra creamy. While everyone was enjoying the last course, there was a knock on the door. Francesco answered. It was Maria.

When the door opened, Maria was embarrassed to see Guglielmo with another family, especially with another woman! She turned around immediately and ran away. Guglielmo asked to be excused and went after her.

"I didn't know you were seeing another woman," she said in a garbled voice through her tears.

Guglielmo quickly explained that he had thought that she was no longer interested in him. He grabbed her passionately and let her tears fall onto his shoulder. After a long silence, he said if she still wanted him, he was all hers. All she could do was cry. She lunged away from him and ran. Now Guglielmo had no hope.

He returned to dinner after wiping tears away. No one asked any questions. Anna, Francesco, Josephina, and Bruno kept the conversation going. As the evening concluded, all lined up to share hugs. The Caparellis were most grateful for the lovely dinner and conversation.

Guglielmo's "family" could not wait to hear what happened with Maria. After the Caparellis left, he described the situation. No one had a good answer as to why Maria was acting so strangely. They advised him to apologize to Mirella for his absence from the dinner table. He did not have to address what was going on, but he should be thoughtful to Mirella.

That night, Guglielmo tossed and turned. He kept asking, *How much do I love Maria?* It was too soon to know if he loved Mirella. She seemed nice. Her father was peculiar, but her mother was cordial. He had not really had time to establish a relationship with Mirella's siblings.

Maria is who I love, but what is she not telling me? She would be a good wife and would keep a neat house. She is a lovely woman, a fine cook, and a devout Roman Catholic. His thoughts flowed in a loop.

Why did she come tonight? Did she want to talk? Maybe she wanted to talk without me there. Could we be happy?

He barely ate breakfast and he had trouble getting through the front door. When Luciano and Maria's brother, Pellegrino, arrived, he could not speak.

Ironically, Luciano was in a good mood, and Guglielmo was not. He encouraged everyone to begin working in their designated areas. Gradually, a thought came to him. If Luciano was in a good mood, he and Maria had agreed that he would ask Maria's father to chaperone them on a walk. At break time, he decided to ask him.

He was not fully prepared to have Luciano say, "Yes."

"When should I come?" he responded with a start.

"How about Sunday after Mass?"

Guglielmo responded as though it was a dream. He was just going through the motions. When his break ended, Mr. Margherita went back to work. Guglielmo needed time to process what had just happened. *Should I be happy or frightened?* He decided he was confused.

At lunchtime, he went to talk with Francesco. As soon as he arrived, he went in the back room to wait for the cobbler. Francesco entered and asked, "What has happened? You look as though you have seen a ghost."

Guglielmo began to explain. "I am supposed to go to the Margheritas' home on Sunday after Mass, but I am afraid that Maria will refuse to walk with me. Should Anna prepare her, or not?"

"Come to dinner tonight and we will ask Anna."

Evening took forever to come. Finally, Guglielmo walked to Francesco's house, stumbling at the door and stuttering when he greeted Anna. She was not surprised he was in a terrible state. Her husband had arrived before the miner.

"Guglielmo, come in and have a glass of wine. You are unraveling, and we need to talk . . ."

Guglielmo politely interrupted her and assured her that he was okay.

"All right then, dinner will be ready in ten minutes."

Francesco began to speak. "Do you love Maria enough to trust that she will open up to you?"

"I have no idea," he said. "The way she has been acting makes me think that she wants me out of her life."

"I don't agree," Anna retorted strongly. "Maria is making herself sick over this. She is agonizing over something. Guglielmo, you have a calming effect on people. Set her at ease. Then, perhaps, she will tell you what is happening."

Francesco agreed. "Let's say a prayer of thanksgiving for our food and ask for patience with Maria."

Over dessert, Francesco consoled Guglielmo by saying, "It is in God's hands now."

Guglielmo had to wait two more days before Sunday. Each night, Francesco had him eat dinner with Anna and himself so that he did not feel alone.

On Sunday, Francesco, Anna, Bruno, and Josephina went to church with Guglielmo. They waited for Luciano and Sebastiana to arrive. Everyone was cordial, so there was some peace in his heart. After Mass, Luciano told him he should come later for dinner and a walk.

No one could figure out what Maria was thinking. As they went their separate ways, a little up the road, Digger stopped them. He said he knew what was ailing Maria.

"I don't believe you," Guglielmo said.

"I will tell you, if you reward me for this information."

"Absolutely not," Francesco barked.

"Don't be too hasty," Digger teased.

They continued to walk home. Guglielmo told Digger to come to the Triolos' house in an hour. "How much money do you want?"

"I don't want money," he said. "I want a job in the mines."

"We'll see you in an hour."

After he left, all five were aghast.

Francesco spoke first. "What kind of worker was Digger when he worked for you, Guglielmo?"

"He was a good worker and quite skilled. His problem was that he wanted to know everyone's business so he had leverage for loans and blackmail. In one instance, his spying on a conversation was helpful. He actually saved a man's life by warning the authorities."

"Does he get the truth, or is he looking for attention?" queried Francesco.

"Most of the time, he's accurate. What are all of you thinking?" Guglielmo asked.

Anna said that "So far, Maria had not wanted to share what has happened."

"Maybe we should hear what Digger has to say and then it might be easier for Guglielmo to ask her directly, instead of asking general questions."

"What about giving him a job?" Guglielmo asked Francesco.

Francesco deferred to Bruno, "What do you think?"

"I think if Guglielmo really loves Maria, then he might investigate what Digger has to say. It's obvious that Maria cannot, or will not, reveal her feelings. If Digger is wrong, he jeopardizes his chance of getting a job. We know he is desperate for employment. He bartered all those loans and people are not paying him back."

Josephina agreed with her husband.

Francesco turned to Guglielmo and said, "If you feel you can keep an open mind to what Digger has to say, then let's consider allowing him to earn some money. If his motive is to stir up trouble, we will know, and he will be the loser. One condition: he needs to know if he meddles into our miners' business and upsets the workers or anyone else, he will be terminated immediately."

"Okay," responded Guglielmo.

There was a knock at the door.

CHAPTER 13

UNITY

E veryone was nervous. Francesco motioned for all of them to walk outside. He did not want to welcome Digger into his home, as that seemed inappropriate at this time.

"Out with it," Guglielmo said.

Digger began. "Some time back at the bar, Mr. Margherita was drunk and began talking crazy talk. In the middle of all that, he sobbed that he had raped his own daughter."

Everyone gasped and there was a long pause.

Francesco came to his senses. "If he was drunk, how do you know he was telling the truth?"

"The bartender said that for a couple of weeks, he came in every night and got so drunk that he had to ask him to leave the bar. In between drinks, Mr. Margherita would cry and tell the same story over and over again."

"Get out of here," Francesco said.

"What about my job?" Digger demanded.

"We need to verify the information first," Francesco said.

"You'll find out it's true," he said, putting his finger in Francesco's face. "I'm no liar. I'll be at work in the morning."

"Not yet," Francesco said. "Go!"

The group went back inside. Francesco turned to the others, not knowing what to say. The ladies were crying and so was Guglielmo. He couldn't bear the thought that someone would hurt delicate Maria, especially her own father.

Finally, Guglielmo spoke. "If what he says is true, it makes sense that Maria would stop wanting to see me and would be too ashamed to tell anyone. If it is true that Luciano did this dastardly thing, it is not Maria's fault. Knowing Maria, she is probably blaming herself."

Anna wiped her tears and added, "Now you know how to deal with Maria. Tell her that you think you know what has happened and that she could share anything with you. She won't agree or disagree with her parents trailing behind. Suggest that you will go to the market and find a private place to talk."

The group had reached consensus, even though they could hardly believe what they had heard. It was time for Guglielmo to leave for dinner at the Margheritas'. Francesco urged him to come back to his house afterward to sleep. No one wanted Guglielmo to stay alone.

With his shoulders slumped and his head hanging low, he slowly left for dinner. He knew that he had to change his mood when he saw Maria. He wrestled with himself, because his first inclination was to punch Mr. Margherita. To keep his composure, he kept repeating to himself that Maria needed him now, more than ever. He arrived at his destination, put a smile on his face, and straightened his shoulders. He handed the Margherita's a bottle of wine that the Triolos and Lorenzos had made. Maria's father had enjoyed it at dinner a while back, with all of them.

Pellegrino and the sisters were happy to see him. Maria initiated a smile but with tears in her eyes. Her brother asked him to play ball with him. He did. Maria was in the kitchen helping Sebastiana. All the while, he kept his mood positive on the outside, even though he was crying on the inside.

The dinner was tasty and the red wine went well with the food. During dessert, Luciano mentioned that the food business must be slowing down considerably. "Maria only makes half of what she used to make."

"Yes," he said. "Since our economy has weakened, business suffers."

He inconspicuously kept his eye on Maria. He offered to help her clean up the kitchen, but her brother wanted him to play with him again. The ladies cleaned. Finally, it was time to take a walk. A shiver went down Guglielmo's spine.

When he thought her parents were far enough away, he said to Maria that she could tell him anything and that he would still love her.

"You don't need to say anything now," he told her. "I can meet you at the market tomorrow, and we can speak privately."

Her hanky was in her hands, because she knew she would need to hide the tears from everyone. Guglielmo would not think of offering a handkerchief to her, because giving a gift of a hanky supposedly brought tears. Because she was already in that mood, the best thing for him to do was to be patient and kind.

She nodded. "Yes."

The rest of the walk was quiet. They walked alongside each other in silence and the looks that they exchanged were lovingly sad. As they arrived at Maria's home, Guglielmo thanked her parents for their hospitality, acknowledging that the dinner had been wonderful. They said their goodbyes.

Guglielmo suddenly arrived at Francesco's. He didn't even remember walking there and he spoke to his friends in a monotone. Yes, he had followed Anna's suggestions. He needed to sleep.

By seven o'clock in the morning, Anna, Josephina, Bruno, and Francesco gathered to support their hardworking friend. He clumsily dressed himself before speaking to anyone. Anna already had breakfast ready.

Guglielmo shared that Maria had a hanky to hide her tears and she had agreed to speak to him in a private area that day at the market.

"When do you ladies take a lunch break?" he asked Anna.

"We usually stop around noon."

Everyone wished each other well and departed.

When Luciano and Pellegrino arrived at work early that day, Guglielmo hid in his office. He could not bear to look at Luciano. With heart pounding, he was ready to go at eleven-thirty. He walked to see Maria. They found a secluded area in the back of all the vendors.

Again, Guglielmo told Maria that she could share anything with him and that he would still love her. At that, Maria gushed with tears on his shoulder. He waited patiently for her to gain composure while stroking her back.

She began, "The most horrible thing has happened. You know that my father drinks too much . . . well, one night he was really drunk when he came into my room. He grabbed me." She couldn't look Guglielmo in the eye, "and had his way with me. I couldn't get away from him, no matter how much I struggled."

Guglielmo kept still, even though he wanted to react. But he could not interrupt her. She needed to get it out.

"When he was finished, he passed out." She paused and wiped a tear. "The next day I told him, 'You have ruined me. No man will want me now.'" He was so upset, he cried; luckily, my mother was not there to hear our conversation. He vowed that it would never happen again.

"I shrieked, 'Then stop drinking!'" She stopped and finally raised her eyes to Guglielmo, her face revealing the repressed anguish.

Guglielmo spoke up. "None of this is your fault. Please don't blame yourself."

"There is one more thing I need to tell you. There is a man named Digger who has been blackmailing me about it. I pay him half of my weekly salary. He comes here to collect every week and sometimes more often. Now he wants more money."

"That's why your father talked about your lower pay," Guglielmo said. "It was going to Digger?"

"Yes," Maria said, her head bowed.

"Don't pay him again. I will deal with him. Stay close to Anna and Josephina. The police chief will help you, certainly."

Maria threw her arms around Guglielmo. "I have been so ashamed. I couldn't even look at you."

"I know, and it has been killing me inside. We'll have Digger arrested. I don't know how you would want to deal with your papa . . ."

"One thing at a time," Maria said.

"Agreed. Let's go to Anna and Josephina for help with the police chief."

"Thank you so much, my love," Maria sobbed.

Shortly after their conversation, Guglielmo rushed to the cobbler shop. Francesco and Bruno were not surprised and closed shop for the day to seek out Digger. They guessed he was in the bar. Francesco said that he would take the lead.

"Digger, we need to talk to you outside."

"Three against one?" he said, to the rest of the people in the bar. "Take notice if I don't come back, everyone."

When outside, Francesco began. "We know you're blackmailing Maria," he hissed. "We can see to it that no one else hires you in all of Palermo."

On cue, the police chief arrived to arrest Digger, and Francesco and Guglielmo helped restrain him. Kicking and screaming, Digger went to jail. The chief would interview the men the next day.

After that, the three men went home. Guglielmo was indebted to Anna for speaking with the chief of police that morning when she delivered his day's lunch. Relieved, Maria broke down with the ladies, who finally could comfort her.

Guglielmo said to Maria, "I've been with my wife before I knew you, so you need not worry if you are not a virgin. Will you marry me, Maria?"

She hesitated and then responded, "There is nothing more important to me than spending my life with you."

Guglielmo's face eased into a smile.

"but . . . ," she continued. Guglielmo's heart nearly stopped. "before I agree to marry you, we must decide what to do about my father."

Whatever you want, Guglielmo thought.

"I don't know what to say to my father. We need to think about this further."

After dinner, Guglielmo and Francesco walked Maria home. As they approached the house, Maria heard her mother screaming. She went into the house and looked through a window; there, before her eyes, was her father hanging from a tree branch in the backyard. She attempted to console her mother. *Now she must never know the secret*, Maria thought.

The men took him down from the tree immediately, so that the rest of the children would not see. The Roman Catholic Church views suicide as one of the worst of all sins—he would go straight to hell. They decided to blame his death on drinking too heavily, which wasn't completely untrue. The men left after Maria's mother was consoled and asleep. Maria was calmed down, after some time.

The next day, Sebastiana went to church alone so she could speak with Father Primo. She lied to him, said that Luciano had died in his sleep, because she wanted her husband to have a church funeral.

After a death in a Sicilian family, there was an outpouring of food, flowers, and money from friends and relatives. During the wake, the body was displayed in their home for three days, in reference to Christ rising from the dead after three days. Family, friends, and even distant kin came to pay respects.

Luciano was displayed in an open coffin, as was the custom. Sebastiana put three coins in Luciano's suit pocket, hoping they would help him go to heaven. The mourners knelt and said a prayer by the coffin. In church and in the procession to the cemetery, relatives and friends were arranged in the importance of closeness to the deceased for the funeral.

Another custom was to pay professional wailers to cry loudly during the duration of the body being displayed and the Mass. The more people wailing—and the louder they were—helped the person into heaven. Of course, Pellegrino and his sisters were crying too. The Catholic Requiem (Funeral) Mass commenced with a cloud of customary incense. Then, Luciano was buried.

One of the conversations that Francesco, Anna, Bruno, Josephina, Guglielmo, and Maria had after the funeral was that of Sebastiana and her budget. Now that Luciano was dead, only Pellegrino and Maria would be financing the family. Josephina suggested that Sebastiana either help her with the laundry or with sewing, after she taught her more about it. The group agreed.

Maria and Guglielmo thought that they could marry in twelve months, so they would not break the tradition of waiting a year after a family member died. Also, Maria said that she would pay her mother a salary for the year. By then, one of Maria's younger sisters would be old enough to become a wage earner. Together, Sebastiana, Pellegrino, and the sister would make enough income to support her mom and her other sibling.

Guglielmo admired how Maria thought about everyone important in her life.

CHAPTER 14

Blessings

Before they knew it, planning time for the wedding arrived. Maria's brother, Pellegrino, was to walk Maria down the aisle, in the absence of her father. Anna was to be the matron of honor. Bruno and Josephina would plan the menu with the two lovebirds. Father Primo scheduled the ceremony for a Sunday in September. It was bad luck to be married in August and on a day other than Sunday.

The ceremony was lovely. Maria's mother and siblings joined the wedding party for the ceremony. The wedding dress was white, but she wore no veil because she was not a virgin. Her mother was ashamed, but Maria couldn't bear to lie in church. Maria's brother played the mandolin and had a nice singing voice. Guglielmo and Maria made a beautiful couple. The food, of course, was delectable.

Guglielmo had saved enough money to buy a little house and a plot of land close to the Triolos and Lorenzos. Anna, Sebastiana, and Josephina made the newlyweds' bed. They added a few coins into the bedding for good luck and strewed rose petals on the bedding. The loving couple did not have enough money to travel for their honeymoon.

One day, thereafter, Anna woke up feeling very sick. It was the first time that she missed work. Then, Anna missed three more days of work. Francesco asked her to go to the doctor.

That night thereafter, Anna had a blessed announcement to make. Francesco was so happy, he literally kicked up his heels and jumped for joy. To no one's surprise, Bruno gave a loud whistle. Josephina, Maria, and her mother made baby clothes, including a new baptismal gown for her.

Four months after Anna's blessed announcement, Josephina and Bruno announced that they had a baby coming, also. Within a month of Josephina's baby being validated, Maria was expectant, too.

As time passed, it was comical to watch the three ladies waddle down the street together. Anna shared her hand-me-down clothes with Josephina, and, in turn, Josephina gave her clothes to Maria. The men strutted like peacocks when walking with their wives. One man asked them if getting pregnant was contagious. Everyone always laughed.

Together with Bruno, Francesco made three pairs of baby shoes and put them in the window of the cobbler shop in order to advertise the wonderful news. Some people tried to buy them, but the shoes weren't for sale. Also, Sebastiana knitted intricate blankets for the infants.

In September, Anna and Francesco had a beautiful baby boy they named Antonino Triolo, after Francesco's father. Soon after, when Josephina delivered, they also had a boy, whose name was Vincenzo Lorenzo. The third baby boy came a month afterward and he was named Daniele Soracco.

The three baptisms were performed on the feast of Blessed Mother Mary's *Assunzione* (Assumption) into heaven on August 15, when she joined Jesus in heaven. It was traditional to dress babies, both male and female, in long dresses that would flow over their mother's arms. Mothers saved the long white gown for future brothers and sisters to be baptized with it and use it from generation to generation.

The entire town of Corleone was invited to Mass and the commemoration, with dinner being served to all. Special guests such as the mayor and chief of police attended. People danced to music for many hours.

CHAPTER 15

LOYALTY

Life was pleasant but barely sustaining. Anna and Maria continued their food business, but they had to cut way back. As agreed, Josephina, along with Sebastiana, washed laundry and made beautiful clothing, but there was less work and fewer sales, now split among more people. The cobbler shop did less business, but the sulfur mines were doing moderately well, because other countries had joined England in requesting sulfur.

In 1890, Francesco paid the Cosca family as paralegals to settle land disputes and provide protection for his land and the sulfur mines so that there would be no hard feelings between neighbors. The economy continued to decline. Soon, no one knew who the Coscas, a mafia family, was protecting. The *pizzu*, (protection money) became so exorbitant that it drained much of Francesco's profits and income. He was not able to pay his employees what they deserved, and though the mines were profitable, because of the ever-increasing protection fees, they were just barely profitable. Nevertheless, his laborers had grown so significantly in numbers in the last few years that they would be able to protect the Triad of Triolo, Lorenzo, and Soracco families, and themselves, if the need arose.

One day, Francesco said, *"Basta!"* (Enough!). He refused to pay the new amount. Thus, the battles began between the Triolo and the Cosca families. Simultaneously, surrounding landowners attempted to take advantage of Francesco's estate.

More men were hired to fight the Cosca clan and the other landowners. Feuds were constant. One type of the *lupara* (for the wolf) machine gun fired round bullets for Christians. For non-Christians, the bullets were square. The *lupara* was mounted on a stand and had a cannon, which had a turn, with a multiple-shot, revolving cylinder. It could fire up to eight or nine rounds per minute.

A notorious soldier, Vito Sangeovese, who had fought with General Provenza, led Francesco's new military force. Vito was an excellent strategist and his men were loyal to him. They were able to protect the Triad.

With the help of General Provenza, he had secured many *luparas*. Sustained fights continued until eventually, many members of the mafia and others were forced to surrender and move away from the area, many to Syracusa, a city on the opposite side of the island.

~ ~ ~

One day, Francesco yelled frantically to Anna, "Hide Antonino!"

Francesco's men again readied their rifles and their revolvers. They were being attacked. Bullets flew. Men fell. Some ran, and others fought. Attackers started fires in the sulfur mines and barn, smoking Anna and Antonino out of the house. They ran to the Lorenzos' house. Men on horses raced through the property with axes and shovels, trying to catch and kill them. But even Vito's wounded men would not stop fighting because of their loyalty to Francesco.

Fathers Marinello and Primo were called to hear confessions and give Last Rights to the mortally wounded, which ensured that the anointed individual would enter heaven directly, instead of purgatory.

~ ~ ~

Francesco needed a break from all the violence. On a cold, blustery day, he went to the town's stables to see if Anna's birthday surprise had arrived, a magnificent Neapolitano horse. Anna had never forgotten those elegant horses they had seen in Taormina on their honeymoon. The beauty was being groomed and would be ready within two hours. Then, Francesco thought he should pay his respects to the mayor.

While in Niccollo's front office, he heard the mayor's conversation with another man. They were rejoicing that they'd had a significant increase in protection fees. When they stopped their conversation, the man started to leave the mayor's office. Francesco saw that it was Mr. Cosca, the extortionist. Francesco hurried away, unseen.

At that moment, Francesco realized that Mr. Cosca had been the competitor who had run up the price against him at the auction and remembered Bruno's question about the mayor's signal to Francesco's opponent. *The mayor would make more money in the long term by receiving protection monies rather than purchasing the mines outright.* He left, infuriated.

He needed to pick up Anna's horse. She was magnificent! The sight of her made him temporarily happy. When she was ready, the stable keeper gave Francesco the saddle, stirrups, and the bridle. He talked to her all the way home.

The horse seemed to understand that she would meet her master soon.

When Francesco arrived home, Anna was in the backyard hanging laundry. He dismounted and called to her. Anna nearly fainted when she saw the gorgeous filly.

"Happy birthday, my love," he said. She began to cry.

Anna said, "Francesco, you are my pillar of thoughtfulness and generosity!" She went to rub the horse's neck and face. "I never expected to have a majestic steed like her. She is spectacular!" The horse bowed her head to receive the affection.

"What will you call her?"

"Precious." It was love at first sight. She mounted the horse and they trotted off.

Francesco's mind returned to the mayor's office. *Had the mayor and the Cosca family anything to do with the murder of our parents? I have to know.*

CHAPTER 16

HONOR

Before the couples knew it, it was time for their three sons to attend school. Antonino fell in love with a striking little girl, Giovanna Cusimano, in the first grade. She became the teacher's assistant in the sixth grade, in 1895, and tutored some of the younger children in reading. She was especially patient with the slower ones. One day, Antonino mustered up enough courage to put a frog in Giovanna's lunch basket. Vincenzo and Daniele couldn't wait to see her reaction.

When lunchtime came, Giovanna went to her lunch basket. The class heard a yelp and then uproarious laughter. To Antonino's surprise, Giovanna looked directly at him and laughed. *How did she know?* From that day on, Giovanna Cusimano, Antonino Triolo, Vincenzo Lorenzo, and Daniele Soracco ate lunch together.

When Antonino and Giovanna were twelve, the families agreed that they should be betrothed. It was customary that the Cusimanos invited the Triolos for a meal to make the betrothal official. Of course, the Lorenzos and the Soraccos were considered family, so they were invited, too. Father Primo, Bishop Lucchessi, and Giovanna's uncle, Cardinal Cusimano, came as well.

The Cusimanos prepared a Sunday lunch after Mass in the vineyard behind their house. There was a very old, enormous tree that provided shade in their backyard. They'd planted various trees around the vines, because each tree enhanced the flavor of the grapes. For example, if a peach tree was near a vine, the grape would have a hint of peach in the wine. There was an ever so slight breeze, with the sun warming the earth. It was easy to drift off in thought about the future.

The Cusimanos had a large extended family, though only one child. The great-grandparents and the grandparents played the accordion, horn, mandolin, violin, flute, and the drum while they sang beautiful, traditional Sicilian songs. When they stopped, Mr. Cusimano proposed a toast to the blessed couple, "Health, wealth, and happiness, with time to enjoy." The crystal glasses clinked in agreement. Antonino put a small gold promise ring on Giovanna's finger. Subsequently, the *antipasti* were served with a *riserva* (quality) red wine. Delicious!

The meal consisted of six courses, with the *antipasti* and the dessert. Goat, veal, pig, and pasta were served elegantly on their finest silver trays.

The next entertainment was all the men singing ancient songs with musical accompaniment. After drinking a little bit more, the giggly women happily sang a little off key. Hugs and kisses were exchanged when saying farewell. It was a special day that everyone would remember.

Over the next years, the four families became inseparable.

After the children graduated from the twelfth grade, Father Guido Primo contacted Francesco and Anna. He, bishop Giorgio Lucchessi, and Cardinal Alberto Cusimano comprised the Pope's selection committee for missionaries who would travel to the United States.

During Napoleon's reign, 1803–1815, the Pope's power had been strong on both temporal and spiritual matters. But having two roles became challenging. Since 1870, the Vatican City State had become reduced to having power only over religious doctrines. Because of this change, Pope Leo XIII wanted Catholicism to expand into new countries, namely America, where it was a very small minority.

The committee had singled out Antonino years before, during his middle grades of school, because of his bravery, intelligence, leadership skills, loyalty to friends, selflessness, and love for the church. The Triolos were honored and thrilled. Few jobs in the area existed, and countless mafia bosses demanded increasing amounts of protection money. Antonino would be able to have a good life away from Sicily.

More children had been born into the Triad, but the holy men proposed to Francesco and Anna that Antonino be the one to attend the university in Sicily to study mathematics and engineering for four years on a full scholarship. When completed, he would go to America, build a basilica, and teach the word of God.

When Antonino heard their offer his brain exploded with questions. Mustering up the courage, he began to speak. First, he expressed how blessed he felt for this incredible offer.

The bishop was an intuitive man, and he wanted to know if Antonino would be willing to take a priest with him to establish a Roman Catholic basilica in America.

"I would love to do the Lord's work, as long as Giovanna is my wife," he told them. The holy men said they would share his conditional response with Pope Leo XIII, and departed.

Francesco sat back in a chair to get comfortable. "You know, the Triolo name has quite a history. 'Triol' was a popular baptismal name with different spellings, meaning 'rock.' When Jesus knew he was going to die soon, He said to the apostle, Peter, 'upon this rock, I will build my church.' The name 'Peter' is translated as 'rock,' as well. Jesus was naming Peter as his successor.

"It has been an Italian tradition to use the grandfather's name as a surname many centuries ago. The familiar ending of 'O' means a member of a family; hence, Triolo means the family of 'Triol' or 'rock.' Later, Triol was a popular name in the Middle Ages. Very few people know that the Triolos are related to some historical leaders. One relative of ours was Julius Caesar."

He was on a roll now. Antonino knew to just listen. "The first Christian Emperor was Constantine l, also a distant relative of ours. I am proud to say that, at the Council of Nicaea in AD 325, Constantine solidified Christian doctrine and stopped the persecution of the Christians.

"Our coat of arms is beautiful. It has a shield with three lions for bravery and three crosses for loyalty. It has a crusader's face armor, and above the armor is a green tree, which symbolizes concern for all of God's resources."

Triolo Coat of Arms

The parents did not know that Vincenzo, Daniele, and Giovanna had been selected for the same reasons. Vincenzo would become the priest for the new basilica, Daniele a doctor, and Giovanna the teacher, if their families agreed. The church would support their education at the University of Palermo and future project, so they were called *prominenti* (elites). It was nearly unheard of to send a woman to the university at this time of history, but Giovanna was so talented and so close to the three men that she was the natural choice. While studying at school, Giovanna would sleep in the nearby convent. The men would stay in the rectory on the university campus and all four would go home on the weekends. They probably would leave for America in four years, when the students graduated.

A year in advance of their trip, the Pope requested that the four families travel to Rome around Christmastime, more than two hundred miles. It would first take several days to reach Palermo by wagon. Then they would travel a few days by boat to the mainland and Rome. They were to spend a few days meeting with the Pope and the planning committee to iron out all the details.

When the date arrived, the 4:00 a.m. departure came quickly. No one slept the night before leaving. They prayed for a safe excursion. Vito Sangeovese was left in charge of their properties, should there be another conflict.

CHAPTER 17

SACRIFICE

The Triolos and Cuismanos readied the wagons in front of *Santa Rosalia* church and met the holy men on the church's front steps. As they traveled northwest from Corleone to the port of Palermo, the poverty became obvious. The land itself had a combination of limestone outflowing, clay regions along the olive trees, and vineyards punctuated it. They smelled garlic in the air.

Daniele, studying to be their doctor, began to speak about garlic. "It is one of the oldest known crops. Its life-giving properties were associated with a supernatural ability to ward off evil forces, even predating Christianity. It appears throughout our medicine and cuisine, let alone our religious traditions, in the use of holy oil, and folklore."

The travelers requested to stop and visit the church at *Monreale*. They were amazed at the grandeur of the mosaic work and were inspired to say a rosary asking God's help for the four chosen ones.

Antonino and Giovanna had been discussing where to go for their honeymoon. When they came to the *Conca d'Oro* (Golden Shell) beach, their decision was made instantly. The soon-to-wed couple spoke softly and giggled together.

Neither could wait for that auspicious day. Just the touch of Antonino's hand sent chills up and down her back. The feeling was mutual for Antonino, as they happily played tag on the beach. They followed a bird's flight, skipping underneath the feathered creature's path, hand in hand.

~ ~ ~

They arrived at the dock. Being the first in line to board the ship, Captain Deanno Graziano welcomed them. He was a jolly fellow with curly black hair and a ruddy complexion. The group thought that he was a rather tall man, until they realized he was standing on a raised deck. Actually, he was only five feet, four inches tall, a *tappo* (a very short man), but he imperially ordered his first mate to get the sailors in position to set sail.

The captain was engrossed in their conversation. They described the mission the four were to complete. Kneeling, he kissed the cardinal's ring out of deep respect and shared that he would pray for them.

He arranged transportation for them to and from the Vatican and for their return to the mainland port from Rome to Palermo. They would need to be picked up at the Vatican on January 2, 1905, at 8 o'clock in the morning, and sail with Graziano.

Deanno escorted them off the boat and introduced them to their Roman guide, Alfonzo Tomassi. Alfonzo was not only a guide, but a cart painter too. Two wagons were waiting for them. The carts had two huge wheels and an open-air top with benches for the riders. Pictures of the grandiose monuments of Rome were painted on the sides. The entire carriage and wheels were painted in bright swirling colors of red, green, blue, and orange. Pulling each wagon were two pinto horses with specially woven blankets, with tassels. Pom-poms of different sizes graced the horses' bridles; colored plumes were attached to the animals' head and hindquarters. As the horses bobbed their head in and out of their food sack, bells would ring.

Buildings were larger; the farms looked different than at home. Roman women's attire was more sophisticated and had more designs and colors than the Sicilian ladies were accustomed to wearing. Monasteries were enormous and grander. Delicious scents wafted through the air from special dishes that the nuns prepared for the priests.

All the while, the group discussed their project in detail: money, supplies, personal necessities, a potential timeline. They were unsure of how much planning the Pope wanted them to do ahead of time.

The carriages passed the Colosseum. Even though the original name was the Flavian Amphitheater, the size of the structure was appropriately called the "colossal." It took ten years to construct on a site named the *Domus Aurea* (House of Gold). This was the political heart of Rome, and it was here that the plot against Julius Caesar was planned in the temple, where he had been deified.

The driver said, "The underground level of the Colosseum had an amazing structure below the arena. The ancient stage machinery had advanced mechanical elevators, trapdoors, and a complicated system of tunnels below the arena that made the Colosseum's illusions possible.

"The Colosseum was the location of the processions, the fanfare, and the battles between aggressive animals and gladiators, where the audiences arbitrarily decided if a gladiator lived or died. After the events, the arena was filled with water to cleanse it from all the blood and to stage naval battles. Roman greatness was demonstrated with the construction of this landmark in its full glory," shared the driver.

While traveling to the next site, they saw a large bronze statue of the mother wolf that suckled Romulus and Remus, mythological founders of ancient Rome. The beautiful Spanish Steps were close by. They were built to be the widest staircase in Europe in the seventeenth century, in a Baroque style.

It was almost dark when they arrived at the Vatican. They were overwhelmed with the beauty and size of it. Saint Peter's Square has an enchanting visual phenomenon. There are four columns, but, if standing in the middle of the square, three disappear and the eye sees only one column.

The Vatican was more mammoth and more beautiful than they could have imagined. Saint Peter could not have possibly known that when he went up to Vatican Hill to be crucified, the site would become the most exquisite church in the world. It had five naves and a façade adorned with intricate mosaics. Michelangelo's 448-foot dome over the basilica was overwhelming.

Cardinal Cusimano was amused to observe their reactions. He had traveled to Rome many times, given his station in life. The group was greeted by several nuns who lived at the Vatican. One was Sister Santina Angelica, who recognized the cardinal and acknowledged him. They were all escorted to their rooms. On the way, they marveled at the Swiss Guard members dressed in their bright uniforms.

In the basilica, the ladies wept when they encountered the *Pieta*, (Statue of the Virgin holding the dead body of

Christ). The Sistine Chapel was resplendent with magnificent paintings on the ceilings and walls depicting biblical stories from the Old and New Testaments. The wonders were intoxicating.

"It's so beautiful that it's difficult to breathe," said Vincenzo.

As they approached Pope Leo XIII the next morning, he welcomed the newcomers with grace and excitement. They had been trained in the correct protocol when greeting his Holiness. Individually, they knelt down, bowed, and when allowed to rise, kissed the Pope's ring.

Following the greeting, the Pope interviewed the foursome. They were everything he hoped for and more, to establish another large Roman Catholic community in the New World. Their faith, strength, love for one another, dedication to others, and courage to work together to fulfill God's mission was evident. After dinner, the Pope announced that he and the cardinals would meet with them several days to plan how the Sicilian foursome would accomplish the goals set out for them.

In the meetings, details were agreed upon for the design of the new church and eventually the grand, domed basilica. Last, the Pope donated a large sum of money for the project, but the group would have to raise additional money to complete the venture.

For the Vatican menu on Christmas day, 1904, favorite foods were prepared for the celebration of Jesus' birth. Recipes were cherished and inherited from ancestors. Some of the dishes were *tortellini* (stuffed pasta cooked in broth), veal marsala, and seven types of fish or seafood combinations. A Christmas salad, *panzanella* , consisting of tomato, bread, fennel (*finoccio*), chicory, celery, green olives, orange slices, lemon juice, and pomegranate seeds was eaten after the main courses.

For the vegetable dishes, they made *copolatina* (eggplant in red sauce flavored with green olives, celery, capers, and garlic), cabbage stuffed with ground lamb, and roasted tomatoes with Italian seasonings, fried peppers, fennel, steamed *broccolini* with olive oil and bread crumbs, roasted white potatoes with Asiago cheese sauce, and baked sweet potatoes.

Buccellat (sweet yeast bread flavored with dried figs, raisins, dates, and almonds), *savillium* (a delicious Roman cheesecake), *torrone* (candy), and focaccia with honey donned the tables.

They were sad to leave the Vatican, but knew there was much to be done in the next year to prepare for their assignment. Alfonzo arrived at exactly eight o'clock in the morning, January 2, as promised. So far, everything had gone smoothly. The travelers did not notice the masked men following far behind their wagons. As they neared the docks, one of the criminals fired a gunshot into the air. The horses reared, and their belongings flew off the carriage. Everyone lunged for the papal money, the criminals included.

"Give us your money," their leader said, brandishing his gun.

"I would rather die than give it to you," Giovanna's father, Alessandro said.

"I can arrange that," the masked leader said, shooting him in the chest. The women screamed and scrambled for him.

"Give it away," Guglielmo said.

"We can't!" Josephina cried.

"If we're all killed," Francesco said, "they won't build the church at all."

Daniele used his foot to shove the wooden box toward the robbers.

Alfonzo had been a part of this rotten deal. He had listened to their conversation on the way to the Vatican. The plan was to attack the Sicilians when they were close to the ship. The scoundrels stole the wagons, leaving the group and their belongings, and charged toward the east.

Stranded with a dying man, they reacted quickly.

"Antonino, run and get the port authorities to follow the wagons," Francesco instructed.

Giovanna flagged down a wagon, explained what happened, and begged the driver to bring her back to the Vatican.

"Daniele, can you do anything for Alessandro?" Guglielmo asked.

"I have no instruments with me," he replied, putting pressure on the wound. "We need to find help."

Anna ran to the nearest onlookers.

Vincenzo guided them in prayer and tried to keep everyone calm.

At the Vatican, Giovanna, out of breath, called for Sister Santina Angelica to take her to the pontiff, who sent out a dozen Swiss Guards to find the bandits. If anyone could find them, it would be them. Giovanna rode with them on a fresh horse so that she could show them the location of the robbery.

The Pope's guards and the port authorities separated to cover more territory. Giovanna's attention was now focused on her father. The doctor had just arrived. In the meantime, Antonino rented rooms at a nearby inn. The doctor had brought a stretcher for all the men to carry Giovanna's father to a bed.

The army of men found the brigands at the Circus Maximus.

"Put down your weapons," a Swiss Guard officer ordered. "Get your arms up."

The criminals were not about to follow orders and fired. Three guards were killed. With no cover to be had at the raceway, the firefight took out members on both sides. After some time, the shooting finally stopped. Unfortunately for the criminals, the Swiss Guard had numbers on its side. Only one criminal lived.

The remaining guards seized him for interrogation.

"Where's the money?"

"You've stolen from the Pope himself!"

He resisted telling them where the money was; but the officers did not relent.

"Do you care nothing for your soul?"

Finally, when the felon was totally exhausted and weary from his wound, he confessed to where the money was, hidden in the west section of the Colosseum. He did not want to burn in hell for all eternity. Weakly, the felon took them to the area.

Back at the inn, Giovanna's father was sallow. She knelt down to pray. Soon, Antonino, Daniele, and Vincenzo came to the room. They knelt down with Giovanna to say a rosary. Her papa moaned all through the night, even though the doctor had given him medication for pain. He had lost a great deal of blood. No one slept that night, fretting over Giovanna's father and how to get him back home. The next morning, the doctor returned to check on him.

Alas, he died in Giovanna's arms. The trip home was extremely difficult. Graziano, the ship's captain, diligently tried to comfort them. When they arrived in Palermo, the body was carried to the wagon returning home.

The trip to America became even more important because no one wanted Alessandro to die in vain.

CHAPTER 18

CONTENTMENT

Nearly a year had passed, and everyone was in church.

"I pronounce you husband and wife," announced Cardinal Alberto Cusimano. Antonino kissed Giovanna with such love that the families began to cry. The church shook with the attendees' applause and cheering. Giovanna's friend, Adelina, began to sing *"Ave Maria"* ("Hail Mary") as only she could do. Her lilting, operatic voice sent chills down Giovanna's back. Antonino held Giovanna close to him. This was a dream come true. When Adelina had finished her glorious rendition, the newlyweds gleefully floated down the aisle of the *Santa Rosalia* Church.

Antonino and Giovanna Triolo

The entire church was adorned with indigenous flowers. The bride's and bridesmaids' bouquets were made of alpine pansies, trumpet gentians, rosemary, jasmine, bougainvillea, and roses. Giovanna was particularly fond of yellow roses, so her bouquet abounded with them. On the altar, there were huge white baskets filled with flowers. Enormous colorful bouquets were attached to the end of the pews. The groom had an exquisite yellow rose boutonniere, and the groomsmen wore a variety of the lovely flowers. Parents wore different arrangements of the nosegays. There were also elaborately tied ribbons decorating the doorway, symbolizing that, after the couple exited the church, they had "tied the knot." *Benissimo!* (Beautiful!)

After the ceremony, a log had been laid across a stand. Giovanna and Antonino picked up a double-handled saw and proceeded to cut the timber in half. It was an expression of the deep commitment they had to each other in their new partnership. Afterward, the log and saw were left outside the church for all to view as they entered or exited the church.

Giovanna looked so beautiful in her great-grandmother's wedding dress. Three generations of women had worn the exquisite dress. Giovanna, her mother, and her grandmother agreed that after the wedding, they would make heirloom pillows from the dress, as it had had to be mended in many areas because of its age.

The white color of the dress represented purity, and the handmade lace veil represented virginity. The *mantilla* (veil) "saved" the couple from bad luck, because the groom was not supposed to see the bride's face before their ceremony. The string of pearls and earrings that Giovanna wore had been given to her by Antonino's parents, handed down for generations. Giovanna's mamma had also given her a swan's feather to put into Antonino's pillow to prevent infidelity.

Giovanna's great-grandfather had given Antonino his pocket watch. Inside was a picture of his lovely new bride. His new father-in-law had given him ten gold coins. The couple was very blessed, indeed. These coins, and the church money, would take them to America, where their future would be much better than in their beloved, but bankrupt Sicily.

The Triolos and the Cusimanos rejoiced because they were able to give their children a traditional Italian wedding that they'd never had. In a way, this celebration was for all of them, too.

When they entered the church's hall, they viewed an astonishing abundance of food. All of the dishes were the favorites of the bride and groom. Francesco and friends had slaughtered a calf and baked it all night before the wedding. The flower girls circulated with *mortadella*, *calamari*, *prosciutto*, cheeses, potatoes, peanuts, olives, stuffed mushrooms, *antipasti* with salami, and *focaccia*, and bridesmaids came by with homemade strawberry or raisin wine, commonly known as "raisin jack." White raisins had been added to the pressed grape skins and allowed to ferment. Tables brimmed with wedding soup, lasagna, *gnocchi*, penne pasta with sausages, spaghetti and meatballs, and several kinds of roasts with potatoes and vegetables. Sweet and aromatic fruit salads adorned the tables.

The neighbor women had made some of their favorite cookies, such as *cucidati* (fig), *todos* (chocolate cookie balls), *biscotti di pinoli* (pine nut), and *wandi* (donuts), which boded good luck for the new partners. The *cassata* (cake) was beautifully decorated with candies and fruit. One could eat *tiramisu*, *tortoni*, and chocolate *zeppole* (donuts). *Cannoli* (stuffed pastry), a Cusimano family favorite, also had to be there. *Mamma mia!* (My mother!, an expression meaning "Oh my goodness!")

After a lavish multicourse meal, the bride and groom were expected to throw down their wine glasses. The number of shards indicated how many years of happiness the jubilant partners would have together. Glass pieces were strewn everywhere. Frequently someone would yell, *"Evviva gli sposi!"* ("Hurray for the newlyweds!"), and they would have to kiss. They kissed far too many times to count.

Family and friends played the mandolin, horn, *pistolato*, Jew's harp, accordion, and the harmonica. The first dance was for the newlyweds. They were in their own world. Antonino repeatedly recited his wedding vows to Giovanna, as he had done for so many years before. Applause awakened them to the fact that the music had stopped.

Ensuing dances were with Giovanna's parents, grandparents, and great-grandparents. The highlight was when Giovanna's great-grandmother danced with Antonino. Women wept and even the men had a few tears in their eyes. As tradition dictated, the "money dance" was next. During this dance, great-grandpa put a gold coin in Giovanna's bag for good luck. Even though the congregation was poor, they shared what little they had.

Men lined up to take turns dancing with Giovanna while they stuffed money into her satin bag. Women lined up to dance with Antonino, too. Daniele had cut Antonino's tie into pieces and was selling them to the women who danced with him.

After everyone was happy with wine, the traditional music and dance, the bawdy *"C'e La Luna Mezz'o Mare"* ("There's the Moon in the Middle of the Sea"), was played. In it, the daughter asks her mother to choose her husband, but the mother can't decide, because of what men of the different professions would provide for her daughter.

On schedule, *"la tarantella"* ("the tarantula") dance was next. Dancers in groups of four raised their right hands and moved clockwise, skipping and kicking along the way. They then raised their left arms, and everyone danced counterclockwise, repeating the same motions. They also danced the nail, the *polyp, the tarascon, the capona*, and the *fasola*. Using tambourines with the dances was common. Legwork involving heel to toe and toe to heel was mixed in. These dances are lively with skipping, and can be danced with or without a partner. Rotating circles clockwise and counterclockwise is traditional. Forming a bridge with two lines of dancers arching their arms while some of the dancers danced "under the bridge" gives a nice variety of movements. Young and old alike joined in.

Next, Giovanna's great-grandmother, grandmother, mother, Isabella, Anna, Josephina, Maria, and other female adults sang several cherished traditional Italian songs. The audience whooped and hollered *"Benissimo! (Beautiful)"* The men, not to be outdone by the women, came together and sang Italian love songs. Wine glasses throughout the room lifted often in honor of the bride and groom.

An older widow then began the "broom dance." She picked up a broom and started dancing in the center of the room. Everyone encircled her. The young women were careful not to let the broom touch their feet, because it meant that they would never marry. When she decided to "drop" the broom, she ran for a handsome, young male partner. Everyone else then changed partners, too. Whoever was left without a partner had to pick up the broom and continue dancing with it. When that person dropped the broom, he or she secured a partner, and the process repeated itself until everyone was exhausted and in need of a drink.

Customarily, there was also a "cookie dance." Dancers formed a single snaking dance line around the dance floor and up to the cookie table. But no matter how many times the line encircled the table, it never ran out of pastries. Isabella saw to that!

During the flurry of these activities, it had grown dark outside. The stars were especially brilliant that evening, and the full moon glowed like a fire in the sky. November 5, 1905, had turned out to be a perfect day for the wedding.

Music began again, and the couple started to dance, staring into one another's eyes. *Was this a dream?* No, it was the beginning of their life together and it promised to be extraordinary. God smiled and blessed these two for the exceptional things they would accomplish together, with their friends, in the New World.

The time had now come for the couple to depart from the reception. The guests were given five white, sugar-coated almonds to symbolize health, wealth, joy, fertility, and long life. As Giovanna and Antonino left, the guests gently threw confetti at them, reminding them of the bitterness and sweetness that coexists in life. As the couple was leaving, Antonino's parents, Francesco and Anna, released two gorgeous white doves into the air. The birds embodied the ideas of monogamy, love, and happiness. The group yelled *"Per Anni!"* ("For a hundred years!") to the couple as they stole quietly away into the night.

That evening, they checked into a small inn. Within an hour, the manager came running, thinking that someone needed medical assistance because of the noise coming from their room. Antonino had to awkwardly explain to the manager that it was their honeymoon night. The manager said, "Mamma Mia," simply smiled, reminiscing about young love.

The happy couple spent a few days at *Conca d'Oro* (Golden Shell) beach in Palermo, euphorically in love.

CHAPTER 19

SETTING SAIL

G iovanna and Antonino needed to continue preparing for their voyage to America. Cardinal Cusimano knew bad weather was coming soon, so he had chartered a reasonably priced ship to take Giovanna, Antonino, Daniele, and Vincenzo to America shortly after the wedding in early November 1905.

The SS *Vincenzo Florio* was to be their temporary home. Because the ship was much smaller than most, it traveled at nine knots instead of the typical twelve knots on larger ships. There were clipper bows, one funnel, three masts, and an iron hull. It had a single small-screw propeller that helped the ship turn when necessary. It was about five hundred gross tons and one hundred feet long. Most other ships transporting people to America were at least three thousand gross tons and four hundred or more feet long. After arriving from its builder in Glasgow, its maiden voyage had been on March 29, 1880, from Florio, Palermo, to America. The trip was 5,470 miles. It would take 608 hours, or about twenty-six days, if all went well. It was destined to make a total of twenty-nine voyages to America before it would be sold to *Navigazione Generale Italiana* (General Italian Navigation).

Ship accommodations were designed for twenty first-class passengers, twenty-four second-class passengers, and about one hundred third-class passengers in steerage.

Because the ship was smaller and less luxurious when compared to most other ships going to America, there were only five first-class travelers and no second-class passengers. It was primarily the third class that filled the ship.

It was regrettable that Giovanna and Antonino's cherished Sicily could not provide them with a fruitful life. Their beautiful Corleone would have to remain a memory. They had to fulfill the promise they had made to the Pope and cardinal.

The married couple spoke about their concerns regarding their families remaining in Corleone. Giovanna's parents had made a lot of money from the salt fields. Everyone needed salt for food preservation, flavor, and medicinal reasons. Giovanna's father had been so successful that the family business had grown to four times the size it had been in his great-grandfather's time and two times larger than his father's business. How long could her family defend their rights as salt miners when the Mafia was becoming so powerful?

Antonino's family businesses were mainly centered on shoemaking, sulfur mining, and agriculture. Sulfur was as important as the salt business. Until 1900, Sicily produced the most sulfur in the world. Dozens of mines appeared between 1770 and 1900. According to the Ancients, sulfur, or brimstone, curiously, was thought to fuel hell. It became widely used as the need for gunpowder increased and the Industrial Revolution began in America. The Triolos hired more and more workers for mining, but many of them had to be trained as soldiers in order to maintain their business.

Five years before the wedding, Giovanna, Isabella, Giovanna's grandmother, Anna, Josephina, and Maria had begun the process of preparing them by starting fruit trees, so they would bear fruit upon their arrival in America. They planted dwarf lemon and lime trees in pots to prevent scurvy on the journey, as well as making salami, wine, and cheeses. Seeds were carefully packaged for the village men and women to put in the hems and seams of clothes, bags, and hats. Closer to their journey, they compiled staples of oil, vinegar, sugar, coffee, and flour. Quantities of canned and pickled fruits and vegetables needed to last them months, until they were established in America. Preparation of that food occurred before their trip, spring through harvest, week after week.

While Giovanna and her female relatives were preserving food, Antonino and Daniele were planning which animals to hunt and cure. Chickens, pigs, turkeys, cows, goats, sheep, and deer would all be part of the fare. The pelts were given to Francesco. Because preservation of food was so critical, Giovanna's family would provide the necessary salt. Vincenzo would be responsible for bringing wine, fresh water stored in barrels, and the papal money.

The sailing date seemed to come too soon. Leaving family was extremely difficult, no matter how much they tried to prepare. The foursome thought they would never see their beloved families or their revered Sicily again, but their devotion to fulfilling God's plan and to honor Giovanna's slain father, were their driving forces. Sad, the four walked to the dock to board the ship. Their families gloomily said, *"Buon Viaggia!"* ("Have a good trip!") They all tried to be strong as tears invariably emerged.

While the captain prepared the ship for its voyage to America, it made groaning sounds and belched out black smoke. "Lift the anchor," the captain called to the first mate. "Set sail!" Slowly, the ship left the dock.

Passengers viewed the Sicilian shoreline gradually getting fainter. As their homeland disappeared from sight, silence overtook those on the deck. *Pezzo di cielo* (heaven fell to earth) is how they described their beloved Sicily. Here and there, people sniffed and tried to choke back tears. Then, a little quiet crying rippled through the crowd. Then, a sob stuck in someone's throat a little louder than intended; a baby wailed and the sobbing flowed forth among the passengers. They collectively prayed for strength, wisdom, and enlightenment. In unison, they brokenly sang the Italian national anthem.

Slowly, as the crying began to stop, people started to focus on the ship's accommodations. Their sleeping quarters were appalling. They were all crammed into a much smaller area than what they needed, as the other half of the lower level of the ship held all their food and supplies for the trip. No decencies of life or privacy were to be had in steerage and universal needs such as space and sleep were afforded in a miserly fashion. Hanging blankets separated the sleeping areas for the families or couples, the single men, and the single women. The floor had bunks spaced close together and hammocks hung above them. Multiple people slept per bunk or hammock. It was demoralizing; it was dirty, and it smelled foul, as no air vents brought in any fresh air. Because of the lack of ventilation, most people crowded on deck to breathe fresh air during the day.

That evening, Captain Marcello Scardino introduced himself and his small staff to his guests. He explained that because his vessel was much smaller than most ships going to America, they had fewer sailors. "This will be a voyage in which everyone helps, meaning that all of you will have to help me and the sailors when needed. That includes cooking your own food and cleaning your own quarters. Are there any among you who can organize the duties and determine who is responsible for each task?"

Daniele nominated Antonino and Giovanna. "They are our leaders," he said. They told people of their papal mission to establish a church and community. About half of the people in steerage had family already in the United States and had a place to go upon arrival or were heading west, but the other half would join the four missionaries. Giovanna took down the names of the volunteers and composed the schedule of who did what and when, and Antonino presented it to the captain the next day.

Giovanna asked Captain Scardino if she could conduct school five days per week or more, if passengers wanted it. Except for the foursome, who came from prosperous families and could thus attend school, all the passengers were illiterate. Giovanna was determined that everyone be able to read and compute on some level when landing in the New World. All age groups were invited. Because he had only a few years of school, the captain asked to join the class.

For the passengers, it was their first introduction to school learning. Most Sicilians were agricultural workers, not from wealthy families, so school was not a priority.

Unfortunately for most, it would be the only schooling they would ever have. Vincenzo would teach the beliefs of the church; Daniele would instruct on the basics of art and science; Antonino would teach math, and Giovanna would teach Italian, reading, and English.

That first evening, the nascent community organized the volunteer cooking group and decided to pool their food for the journey. The people involved were Giovanna; Nunzio, the butcher, and his wife, Cuncetta; along with Giuseppe, the baker and fisherman. They prepared a beautiful dinner for everyone. They began serving the pasta *sciutta* with pesto sauce of basil, olive oil, pine nuts, and lots of grated Romano cheese, potatoes, and string beans to a very hungry and weary group. The foursome had eaten a light breakfast very early that morning so were famished by dinnertime.

Vegetables had been sautéed with a little olive oil and onion. Some mixed the vegetables with their pasta. Fresh fruit salad was soon depleted. The green salad came later in the meal. Last, but not least, Giuseppe and his group brought out the hot *todo* cookies and amaretto cake.

Starting off with wine on an empty stomach, the effects of the liquor were greater than usual. Late in the evening, Daniele suffered adverse effects from the wine and the rocking of the boat. Standing at the edge overlooking the water, he lost his balance and fell overboard.

CHAPTER 20

SELFLESSNESS

"Man overboard! Man overboard!" shouted the captain.

Antonino jumped into the angry water without a thought for his own safety. He had been a swimmer since he was four years old, but he had never experienced such a treacherous body of water. Giovanna waited on the deck impatiently with tears in her eyes. She loved the men so much.

Antonino felt the water pull him in a completely different direction from Daniele. He swam desperately, with wide, broad strokes. *Focus, focus*, he kept repeating. He struggled toward his friend, gulping in water, as he was pulled under. Praying that he could muster up the strength, he realized that he was near the top of the waves. Sharks frequented these waters.

Focus, focus, he reminded himself again, as he continued to pray. Finally, his head bobbed out of the water. Now able to make some headway, he swam toward Daniele, only to be bumped off track. At least two sharks surrounded him.

Sharks have poor vision. They encircle something to determine whether it is food. Antonino moved closer to Daniele. Diving once more under the water, he saw his friend motionless beneath him. Antonino grabbed him and surfaced. The sharks swam in closer. Frantically he kicked back to the ship.

Meanwhile, the captain was bringing the vessel as close as he could, while other passengers readied the nets. Vincenzo dove into the water and grabbed Daniele who gave a startled scream. A large net vaulted over his head. The men quickly hoisted Daniele into the ship with a pulley. Antonino and Vincenzo climbed into the boat as blood gushed over their arms and face. A shark had bitten off Daniele's left leg up to his knee. He was so weak that he could barely reach for the sailors when they pulled him on the deck.

Giovanna rushed to Antonino, who climbed aboard and lay flat on his back, resting on her lap and gazing at the blackened sky. A lightning bolt cracked like the whip his father used to train Precious, Anna's Arabian. He drifted off from exhaustion, for what seemed like only a moment.

Almost all the passengers were on one side of the ship trying to view the action while others were attempting to pull the sharks into the boat with the nets. The craft was nearly on its side.

"All of you," a crewman yelled at the gawkers. "To the other side, lest we capsize!" Half of the crowd panicked and ran to the other side.

As the wind howled, hail began to beat on their skin.

The men hauled up the nets and stabbed and clubbed the creatures, screaming "Die, monster, die!" Men jabbed a torch into a shark's mouth. After more clubbing and fire, the animals finally died. Dinner for the group! The amount of meat on the sharks, after butchering, should feed them for some weeks. They celebrated as victors for capturing the vicious predators. While butchering a shark, they would recover Daniele's leg, and Vincenzo would be able to give it a proper burial at sea.

When Antonino regained consciousness, he grabbed onto Giovanna's arm to lift himself up. It was then that he discovered what had happened to Daniele's leg. Horror and sadness filled his heart upon seeing his friend. Then he gathered his wits and got some fresh water for the patient to drink. Several people tried to clean the wounded leg. Daniele started to cauterize his own leg, wrapping it tightly and treating it with whiskey and salt to stop the bleeding. He passed out before he could finish the job. Rosina Quattrone stepped forward and told Antonino and Vincenzo that she was a nurse. She finished the job. Back home she had nursed her father back to health after he'd been injured hunting, but Daniele was her first patient who had lost a leg.

Later, Giovanna made hot broth for him, her husband, and Rosina. Vincenzo and Antonino changed the bandages and offered him drinks throughout the night. They slept in shifts, watching over Daniele. His moans and groans continued through the night. Antonino prayed again. High fever plagued the wounded man for the next forty-eight hours.

Because of Rosina's diligent care, gangrene never set in. After a long while, Daniele was lucid and showed delight whenever she offered to be his nurse.

The truth of the matter was that Daniele had noticed Rosina when boarding the ship. She had long, silky brunette hair; glistening dusky olive skin; and lovely hazel eyes. She had worn a bonnet with a large lavender bow and carried a basket for her meager belongings. She had stood aboard the ship as they had sailed away from shore, waving to her weeping mother. Everybody on the floating vessel had felt similarly when they had realized they were braving a new chapter in their lives. These pioneers knew that life would no longer be the same. How different was yet to be discovered.

CHAPTER 21

CONSIDERATION

Each day Daniele became more determined to walk again. Paolo Nero had been a carpenter in the old country, so now he carved a rough cane and a wooden leg for his friend.

On one fine day, when the ship was about halfway to America, Vincenzo and Antonino were talking to the captain. He had been sailing ships to America for the last few years. Death, childbirth, scurvy, and various other illnesses had all been experienced on his voyages.

He told Vincenzo and Antonino that he felt it was his responsibility to help Sicilians traveling to America in any way he could. He firmly believed they could find a promising life there. Vincenzo jokingly asked the captain if the streets were lined with gold, as he had heard someone say.

Laughing, the captain replied sadly, "No, but, I can tell you that if you work hard, it will pay off. You could start your own business and plan it any way you want. You could make a good living for yourself and your family."

"Where do we go first?" Vincenzo asked.

"I will take you to a place in New Orleans, where people will welcome you into their home and cook for you," said the captain. "You can pay for your room and board by working for them in the sugarcane fields. You will even earn a little money to start building your future."

"Wonderful," Vincenzo exclaimed. "I can't wait!"

Antonino began to play his mandolin. Giovanna and the other passengers encircled him to join in on an old song that was a Palermo favorite. People sang with gusto, smiling at beautiful memories of their homeland. Some thought about their betrothed back home; others thought of their family or their small sons and daughters left behind until they could establish a home.

Parents were remembered lovingly, as though the travelers were still working the vineyards, milking the cows, chasing the chickens, cooking delicious meals, laughing, dancing, going to church, and carrying out their regular routines. Nothing is more important to an Italian than family. *Mia famiglia e tutti!* (My family is everything!) Only God held higher priority.

Antonino thought of the first time he had seen his gorgeous bride to be. It had been the first day of school, first grade. From that moment he had known that he loved Giovanna.

She was like no one else. She had fiery determination in her brown-green eyes, and was lion-hearted, like his mother said he was. Her smile spread throughout any room she entered. Intelligence and a sense of humor were only some of her qualities; the rest of Antonino's list was seemingly endless.

About five years ago, after the meeting with the holy men, Antonino ran to school the next day to talk to Giovanna.

"I have so much to tell you after school, by our lake," he said.

"Me, too!"

Neither one could concentrate on their schoolwork that day. It felt like three days had passed while waiting for 3:00 p.m. The teacher had to direct Giovanna in her responsibilities every hour or so, because her mind kept wandering. At the same time, Antonino was a wreck. *What if she wouldn't want to go with him?* At last the clock struck three. The lake felt like it was hundreds of miles away as they ran to it. Finally, they sat by the water, and Antonino described what had happened the evening before.

Giovanna listened. Even though they were already betrothed, Antonino declared his undying love to Giovanna and his intention of having her as his wife. When he finished talking, he asked her if she would consider living with him in America.

"Before I answer, I have to tell you my story," she said.

"Giovanna," he began, "please don't change your mind about our marriage. My heart can't bear it."

Giovanna began to laugh.

How could she laugh at a time like this? Does she not know how serious I am? This is the rest of our lives.

Giovanna started talking, but he couldn't hear her. She stopped and asked if he was listening. After a moment, she began shaking him.

"What?" Antonino said.

"Take a deep breath and listen to me. I was telling you that Father Primo, Bishop Lucchessi, and Cardinal Cusimano came to speak to my parents last night."

"Oh no," Antonino sighed. He still could not grasp why she was so jovial.

"We have watched you grow into a devout Roman Catholic who has exhibited strength, intelligence, selflessness, and a pure heart," she reported them saying. "You are capable and willing to help others." She described her parents asking if they had picked her to do the Lord's work, and they said, "Yes." Her parents had looked at each other and smiled.

"Giovanna, baby," her mother began, "we have prayed for so long that you would have more opportunities than what we can offer you. Our life has been difficult. It would be our greatest joy to have you fulfill such a great destiny."

"We cannot tell you how much we love you," her father continued, "and how proud of you we have always been. You are a very special child sent to us, and we knew you would do important things for the Lord. We figured if we could only have one child, she would be extremely special, and you are. God will show us the way until we die."

"Oh no," Antonino moaned. "Do they want you to enter the convent?"

"No. Please listen to me," Giovanna said, more calmly now. Antonino tried to compose himself.

"The bishop asked me what my intentions were," she said, "showing how she straightened her shoulders, cleared her throat and spoke. "I said, 'My desire is to serve the Lord and to help others—with Antonino.'"

Antonino was astonished that she had been so bold.

"They offered me a scholarship to the University of Palermo to become a teacher!" The offer was highly unusual because girls were not invited to the university unless they had a great deal of money or had expressed interest in becoming a nun. "I was so relieved, Antonino. I have no intention of becoming a nun!"

He jumped up, pulling her toward him, began to twirl her in a dance, and started to sing. The love in her eyes was overwhelming, and they both began to cry joyfully.

"You are my soulmate pillar," she said.

Antonino let out a loud, joyous whistle, as only Bruno could have taught.

"Let's remember everything about this day," she said. "Listen—hear the white-winged larks, sand martins, and red-rumped swallows? Look—see the lake creatures swirling in the water." A blue, gold, and red dragonfly circled her head. She extended her hand, where the creature landed briefly. It flitted away to eat tiny insects and landed on the surface of the water. Suddenly, a fish broke the surface and ate it in a flash.

They simultaneously crossed themselves on behalf of the dragonfly. It had had a short life, but a purposeful one, as it worked to keep the population down of the insects it ate; itself became food for the fish. She knew that this was a sign they would accomplish their goals, that they had a small, but significant part to play in God's larger plan.

The couple decided to go to the *Santa Rosalia* Church with their rosaries and pray about their upcoming journey.

CHAPTER 22

OPTIMISM

The passengers had sung many favorite songs with Antonino. He stopped to rest. As he gazed at the starboard side of the ship, he saw Rosina helping Daniele walk with the wooden leg and cane. People in the crowd turned their head to see him making his way to Vincenzo. Applause resounded.

Daniele and Rosina beamed. They made quite a handsome couple. Rosina requested that Antonino lead them in singing the Italian National Anthem. The crowd stood up and joined in singing. A group dynamic had been developing among the travelers, and at that very instant, they felt like a family with a single plan: to have a more prosperous life than they could have in the old country.

Suddenly, the din of their singing was interrupted by a cry for, "All men on deck." The captain was sharply turning the ship.

"Women below deck!" he commanded. Women grabbed for children's hands and ran toward the ladders to go below.

Seemingly out of nowhere, a cannonball flew over the deck of the Italian ship. Pirates! The confused male passengers followed the lead of the sailors.

"You there," a crewman shouted toward Antonino. "Gather the men and bring up the munitions!"

Captain Scardino's first cannonball hit the pirate's port side. The enemy ship teetered and tottered but began to stabilize. Under the first mate's orders, the Sicilians launched another cannonball. This time it missed. They loaded again, but before the third cannonball could be fired, an incoming cannonball struck. It was high in the air, but destroyed the lead mast. As it collapsed, seven passengers were caught under it.

Their third cannonball navigated to the opposing vessel as the pirate ship came closer. It was a direct hit to mid-ship. The pirates began abandoning their vessel. The only safe place in the Atlantic was now the immigrants' ship.

Direct hit. Debris, people, wood, clothing, and animals floated in the sea. "Strong men, we need to move this mast!"

"Find the priest," a person shouted.

It had started so suddenly and had been over in an instant, almost as if the attack had never happened. The people who died under the mast, though, were a grim testimony to the reality.

Vincenzo joined in with the rest of the men to free the bodies pinned under the mast. When things had settled down, the passengers wanted to pray, showing their gratitude that the ship was still floating toward their destination and that more people had not been killed.

Vincenzo went below. Shortly he returned with his Bible and got out his rosary beads. Some were weeping and praying; others knelt in shock at the passing of their loved ones. They had known this trip would have its share of hardships, but pirates? It was a formidable reminder of how fleeting life can be and how important it is to share love and kindness with others every day.

Next, they had to decide what to do with the seven dead bodies.

"If we bury all seven of them at sea," remarked Captain Scardino, "and they are too near our ship, the sharks will get too close to us."

The captain and first mate asked for volunteers to take the bodies in a rowboat and dispose of them a safe distance, as well as, pick up flotsam. It would be very dangerous, and those who volunteered would have to row the boats quickly away from the burial site to avoid the sharks, which they hoped would be distracted by the pirates in the water.

Unfortunately, many of the men were spooked by the pirate attack, but Antonino knew it was the right thing to volunteer. Giovanna would follow her dear, brave husband to the ends of the earth, if he were going there, so she volunteered, as well. Then Vincenzo, but Antonino refused to allow them to go. "You are needed to console those in mourning, and the ship needs its priest," he said.

Daniele volunteered to go, but no one wanted him to potentially lose another limb—or his life. "Even a quick burial of the bodies needs a priest to oversee it," Vincenzo insisted. Antonino knew better than to argue with his priest.

The captain told Antonino, Vincenzo, and a crewman to go out about a half mile, if possible, starting their boat from the other side of the ship, away from the pirate wreck.

He warned him to not take any unnecessary risks. If they saw any sharks, they were to turn back.

If only it were that simple, Antonino thought. They stepped into the lifeboat, and the sailors lowered it by pulleys while Giovanna, Daniele, Rosina, and the others prayed.

They began to swiftly row. *Was this really happening?* Antonino thought. *I never would have imagined this responsibility on the ship. But I know I'm doing the right thing.*

It took them about half an hour to get to a spot that was far enough away from the ship to cast the corpses. The boat rocked to and fro, and a little bit of water seeped into the lifeboat. One body fell overboard without assistance. They prayed for their souls, as they gently committed one and then another to sea. *So far, so good*, Antonino thought. He watched as the bodies sank into the depths of the sea while praying.

The ship looked so small, so far away. The sea had grown more restless. A storm brewed in the distance. The waves slapped and knocked against the boat, making rowing arduous. The thunder was getting closer and the lightning snapped above. *Was that a shark's fin?*

Vincenzo implored *Santo Leoluca*, one of the patron saints of Sicily, for protection. *Santo Leoluca*, born in Corleone, was credited for saving the city of Corleone during the outburst of the plague of 1775. The venerable man had healed the sick, exorcised demons, raised paralytics, and counseled the lost toward salvation at the Monastery of Mount Mula.

They lifted another stiff body and lowered it into the water. The last corpse was the most heart-wrenching. She had just had a baby girl, Sophia, four months ago, and the baker and fisherman, Giuseppe, was the father.

Right now, they needed to stop thinking of each individual dead person. Instead, they needed to row away from the sharks. They rowed as though they were in a race. Vincenzo noticed something else in the water. *Was it another person? No, goats!* Several goats were treading water near a large floating piece of the pirates' ship. "Save the goats," he cried, and they pulled them into the lifeboat. "Blessed be the Lord."

Antonino then saw that there were two chests floating atop a large flank of boards. He reached for a chest. Suddenly, a shark jumped out of the water. The creature missed him and slammed back into the sea. In its landing, it discovered a body, which momentarily distracted it. They hurried their strained efforts to capture the first chest and get it into the boat.

They lunged for the second chest. Getting a grip on it, they lifted it into the lifeboat.

"We must get back to the ship," Vincenzo said. It was a good thing Antonino, Vincenzo, and Daniele had raced boats in the lake back home.

A leak sprang in the side of the boat. *No, not now!* Antonino thought. Water began trickling in slowly, and it gained momentum as the two heavy chests weighed the tiny craft down. To stay focused, they pretended they were gaining speed toward the finish line. They could just about hear the crowd cheering.

Finally, they made it back. Crewmen elevated the lifeboat to the ship's deck by pulley, and before they knew it, they were being hoisted into the ship. Antonino heard the goats bleating and people clapping and asking what was in the chests, as he collapsed into Giovanna's loving arms.

CHAPTER 23

CAMARADERIE

The captain called everyone on deck to order and to stand back. The boxes had metal locks, so Captain Scardino used a handgun to blow off one of the locks. Antonino knelt down and slowly opened the top only to quickly close it. The crowd gasped. *What was in there?* Giovanna peeked and she began laughing loudly. The curiosity was getting the better of all of them. Antonino let out a loud Bruno-type whistle and couldn't hold back his laugh. The box was full of fine French women's undergarments, much different than everyday bloomers.

He flung them into the crowd and jokes flourished among the men. One of the men, Placido, put some panties on his head, held a corset to his chest, and paraded around the deck. Eventually, the laughter calmed down, and they could focus on the rest of the container's contents.

Next, were a number of books, a Bible among them, and maps of the world; also, construction tools—the crowd became excited. There were also letters in a leather wrap addressed to people in the New World, but the amount of decipherable text was questionable.

Antonino, Giovanna, Daniele, and Vincenzo were the only Sicilians on board who could read and write in both Italian and English. At the very bottom of the case were butcher knives and a hunting gun. By now, daylight was almost gone because of the coming storm, so the group decided to open the second chest the following day, even though everyone was anxious to know what was inside.

~ ~ ~

Captain Scardino rang the bell with the first streams of daylight. The passengers congregated on the top deck. "Where are my swimmers?" he asked. Valuable pieces of wood floated nearby that could be used to repair the mast. Several men were selected to go with the first mate to capture the wood. Meanwhile, breakfast was being prepared by Giovanna, Nunzio, Cuncetta, Giuseppe, and the rest of the cooking group. Giuseppe tried to keep busy by putting his grief over his wife into his baking. *But how can I take care of Sophia myself?* he wondered. *A baby needs a mother.*

Daniele was notably better. His leg was healing well under Rosina's care. As time went on, it became obvious that they adored one another. They would sit together for hours, just laughing and joking. Other times they spoke very quietly and seriously. Sometimes they played games with other passengers.

Playing cards and dominoes were a favorite pastime among the travelers. The most popular card game tournaments were organized by Placido, playing *Scala (ladder)*, *Quaranta (forty)*, *Scopone (related to Scopa)*, *Scopa*, and *Briscola (trick taking game)* and domino game *La Luna* (The Moon). The team with the most points would win that tournament, and then players would rotate teams, to keep the games friendly.

As people formed closer relationships and were more comfortable with each other, the games became more competitive. On paper, the participants were starting to owe hundreds of dollars to each other, with which they'd taunt each other.

Placido often formed a group for a scavenger hunt, hiding some objects in the stored grain or in the wine decanters. Once, the captain was given an apple for each pocket. Anybody who discovered them was allowed to eat them. The only way the apples could be found was by direction of getting "warmer," or closer, to the object or, if they were getting "colder," or farther away from the object.

The addition of goats to the ship meant they could have fresh milk every day. When supplies ran low, adults would drink clabber, which is unpasteurized milk that eventually curdles into a yogurt-like substance. The top priority was to give milk to the baby, Sophia. The rest of the children loved milk, too. Goat cheese would now be an attainable luxury.

Those who knew how to work with wood volunteered to complete the mast, with Paolo taking the lead. They used the tools found in the first chest and the ship's tools. Before they began, they consulted with the captain and Antonino and asked for their instructions, as he was an engineer.

While this job was being completed, passengers had to be careful not to have too many people on one side or another, lest they capsize. Placido made sure that they were both entertained and safe. Antonino and Giovanna held hands, observing their friends playing games.

"I do not care what challenges we are presented with," Giovanna said. "I will not be afraid, because God gave me you, my darling."

Antonino smiled and repeated his wedding vows to her while hugging her. Daniele and Rosina watched them. They turned to each other and looked at one another with tenderness and respect.

Antonino said, "You are my pillar of support."

Many men were needed to lift the mast. Paolo, as the most experienced carpenter, had used rope and special knots to wrap around the mast to lift it. When Antonino gave the signal, the men pulled as tightly as they could. The mast was unresponsive. More rope and more men were needed.

A larger group tried again, grabbing the rope with as much gusto as they could. Slowly the mast moved upward. If they could maintain its new position, the carpenters could nail supporting pieces of wood around the mast and thick rope to secure it upright. The ship tossed back and forth and up and down while the men on one side strained themselves to keep the mast erect, while the men on the other side tried to keep the mast balanced.

What teamwork! The passengers were becoming a community and more dear to each other every day. Friendships formed that would last a lifetime. As the group grew more cohesive, people looked to Antonino for leadership. He was trusted and admired for his bravery, sense of logic, wit, kindness, strength, and humor. His knowledge and education were also impressive. Very few single women were on the ship, but they vied for his attention. No matter, his heart was devoted to his beautiful Giovanna.

Giuseppe knew how to use the hunting gun from the pirate ship's chest. It was an advanced gun, but he had crafted one just like it in the motherland. As they neared an uninhabited island, he carefully aimed at a large bird over-head. *Let me find a good woman for Sophia,* he wished. *Let the morning's first bird feed us now and bring her a mother later, too.*

One bullet released and the bird fell to the deck. He was able to get five more large birds. The cooking team got to work quickly. It was amazing how many parents were able to feed their children with the barbequed meat.

With so much happening that day, time went quickly. The light was already growing dim, and the sun was setting. Alas, the second chest would have to wait until the next day.

Below deck, Antonino and Giovanna snuggled together and quietly whispered their burning love for each other.

CHAPTER 24

WONDER

A ntonino lay in bed dreaming of home. He remembered the day that Father Primo, Bishop Lucchessi,
and Cardinal Cusimano had come to his home. He had
been so frightened that they would make him do what he
did not want to do. The holy men had entered the kitchen
with somber faces. His parents invited them to be seated.
Antonino listened intently. The Cardinal began.

"Pope Leo XIII has considered your proposal," he said.
"But there are some details that must be cleared up. We
want you to graduate from altar boy to deacon in the
church. The responsibility that comes with being a deacon
is understanding the full meaning of the Bible and the messages that God has sent to mankind. A deacon must be an
outstanding role model for people, must be able to assist a
priest in consoling others, and he must demonstrate the
righteous road to be taken."

So far, Antonino liked the proposition.

"Furthermore," the Cardinal continued, "in your journey to the New World, we would like you to protect and
assist your fellow priest in building a church, eventually a
grand basilica, forming a close Catholic community, and
spreading the word of God. You and your wife will take care
of the priest with room and board until the rectory is built.

"You will write letters regularly, keeping the Cardinal
informed of your progress. The church will give you a

stipend to help with your responsibilities. If this is something you are willing to undertake, you will receive your scholarship to the university."

Antonino looked at his parents' faces, trying to discern what they were thinking.

"Papa, what do you think?" he asked.

"I believe you have been given the opportunity of a lifetime," Francesco replied.

"Mamma, what do you think?"

"Heaven has smiled on you, my beloved son, our 'lion heart'. We always knew you were destined for greatness."

The Cardinal concurred.

As they concluded their conversation, Mamma invited everyone to her delectable cannelloni dinner.

The morning bell on the ship refocused Antonino to greet the new day. Antonino and Giovanna rose out of bed, looking forward to a fine breakfast. The chickens had laid fresh eggs, and the sun was brilliantly shining. *We must be thankful for our blessings*, he thought.

On deck, Captain Scardino was giving directions. "For the next event," he said, "we will open the second chest."

Antonino opened the second chest and slammed the lid down quickly, pretending to be shocked.

"What color are the nightclothes this time, Antonino?" a man hollered.

The people who had circled around him laughed and pushed him around a little. Even the captain was now prodding him to open the trunk.

This time Antonino was serious. He slowly opened the trunk, perhaps dubious of the contents. What could pirates garner? It was anybody's guess. There was liquor on the top: bottles of rum, and very old scotch in a *capazo* (basket). The crowd cheered. The liquor was handed over to the captain for later.

Antonino shuffled the rest of the items in the chest. To his amazement, he saw gold coins and ingots, chalices, a large crucifix, silver coins, paper money, a sack filled with heirloom jewelry, cobbler tools, and a deed to a large piece of land in the United States. People asked what it was. He shared that it was someone's landholding.

He was unfamiliar with the word. He tried enunciating it. It is land west of De...DeRidder."

The next word was difficult to read. He asked Vincenzo what he thought it was. Due to some water damage, it was slightly smeared. Vincenzo attempted the word.

"Louis...Lou-is-i-a-na. It's Louisiana," he said. "Does that mean anything to anyone here?"

Captain Scardino said, "It is land northwest of the Baldwin Port of New Orleans. When we arrive at the port, we can ask someone who knows the territory." Vincenzo, Giovanna, and Antonino agreed.

There were still other items in the chest. A beautiful wedding dress that had not yet been finished was on top of a sewing machine. This item made the women cry. *A bride who could never wear her dress? Was it because the groom or the bride-to-be had been killed by the pirates?* They suddenly realized that their good fortune was the misfortune of so many other families. A sense of urgency swept through the passengers, and they knelt. Father Vincenzo led them in a prayer for the deceased victims. Antonino asked the group to say a prayer of thanksgiving for the many blessings they had already received.

There was a heavy silence. *Would the future hold heartache or more miracles?*

CHAPTER 25

TEAMWORK

Before the sun rose the next day, the four leaders met on the deck. They were discussing the contents of the trunks and what would become of all of it. Antonino had no intention of keeping everything for himself, as the captain had granted. He was thinking as a community leader, a role the holy men had expected him to fulfill. The Bible, chalices, crucifix, and wine would become Vincenzo's for the church and basilica. The pirate money, money from the new Pope, Pius X, and whatever other necessary money was needed to build the church, was also for their new basilica.

The maps would be used by Placido, so he could scout and organize people. The letters for the New World would also be given to him. They could still be sent on, when they arrived to America. The books would be the beginning of the group's library.

Nunzio had worked with his father, who had been a butcher in Corleone. The butchering tools would be his. Some of the money needed to go to Giuseppe for raising his daughter, Sophia. Paolo, the carpenter, would use the construction tools to build the church, homes, and businesses. The cooking tools would be Nunzio's and Cuncetta's; they would continue to cook for everyone.

As this was being decided, Daniele asked Antonino for a favor. "Rosina is an excellent seamstress," he began. "Is it possible for her to use the sewing machine? She could finish the wedding dress and make clothes for those who need them."

"What a good idea, Daniele!" After a moment's pause, Antonino resumed. "May I ask you what your intentions are with Rosina?"

"I love her," replied Daniele, "but she is very shy. I do not know how to tell her I love her or find out if she loves me."

Both Giovanna and Antonino looked shocked. "Have you paid any attention to the way she looks at you?" Antonino said. "She obviously cares for you deeply."

"Really?" Daniele was happy.

Everyone chuckled and went on with their planning.

"We will need to determine the costs of things in America," said Antonino. "After that, we will create a budget once we know how much money we have. As for the jewelry, it can be discussed at another time. There's no rush for that." The four agreed.

Just then, the captain rang the morning bell and people began appearing on the deck. Nunzio and Cuncetta started cooking breakfast for everyone. Many of the women helped serve the food.

After a satisfying breakfast of eggs, dried sausage, potatoes, and bread, Nunzio approached Antonino.

"May I have a word with you?"

"Of course, Nunzio. Why do you look so sad today?"

"I have bad news. The food is getting low. The men either need to fish more or shoot more birds. The grain and macaroni are almost gone and there is no more fruit. If we slaughter the goats, we won't have enough fresh milk for the children, and no more goat cheese. What should we do?"

Antonino asked Placido to gather everyone on deck. He then asked Nunzio to explain the situation. Before people could panic, Giuseppe volunteered to lead the fishing. Enough men volunteered. The group was to be ready at the crack of dawn the next day. The nets had been repaired from the sharks and checked for strength.

On the largest net, weights had been added to the bottom. It was funnel-shaped, narrowing at the end. The trick was to gather enough volunteers to lift the netting back on the boats. The weight of the fish would be the challenge, that is, if they were lucky enough to catch them in the first place. They had to trust that God would not let down his disciples.

It was a ferocious night. The ship veered right and left, up and down. Rosina organized caregivers, who frequently emptied the "honey pots" used for elimination, as more and more people became seasick.

The sun was vaguely rising in the east. Some of the volunteer fishermen were still sick, so Giuseppe had to settle for just a few strong men. Desperate for extra help, Giuseppe turned to some of the women, including Cuncetta, Giovanna, and another passenger named Angelina. She had hoped that by volunteering to help fish, Giuseppe would notice her. While caring for the baby, she had fallen in love with Sophia and truly admired Giuseppe.

Giuseppe readied the volunteers. On the count of three, they were to drop the nets, wait for tugging, and then lift the nets back onto the vessel. The first attempt was unsuccessful. Several people got hurt as they crashed into each other. The second try was more organized, because they knew what to expect; they captured three sharks, two large, and one medium-sized.

Those who were not sick cleared the nets and began beating and stabbing the sharks. Others tried to hold the net, even the captain and first mate. One of the larger sharks ripped a significant hole in the side of the net. Giuseppe stuck a club that was on fire in the mouth of the largest one. It took a few minutes for the shark to die. In the meantime, the medium-sized shark perished. With the last of its strength, the third shark snapped at the net while the people were hitting it. Nunzio rendered the fatal blow.

Paolo, Nunzio, Cuncetta, Giuseppe, Angelina, Daniele, Rosina, Giovanna, Vincenzo, and Antonino began gutting the sharks. Paolo and Angelina were newcomers to the cooking group. The group butchered the flesh into steaks and edible pieces and lit a large, controlled fire. They doused the meat in some olive oil and vinegar to tenderize it, and they sprinkled it with basil, oregano, salt, and thyme. The seasick passengers continued recovering, and as a result, everyone had a full stomach.

After the rum and the meal, Antonino started playing his mandolin and Placido harmonized with his squeeze-box. Because of the "liquid courage" with the meal, Daniele asked Rosina to dance. The group started singing and dancing the tarantella. Very happy now, the team volunteered to fish with Giuseppe again. The camaraderie had heightened.

Angelina gazed into Giuseppe's dark brown eyes with great admiration. Giuseppe had impressed everyone who joined in the shark fight. Suddenly, Giuseppe noticed Angelina looking at him. He pretended to wonder if she was the lady who had cared for Sophia. He shyly thanked her for caring for his daughter.

"I really enjoyed it," she said. "I have always dreamed of having a baby girl someday."

An embarrassing pause ensued. They bid an awkward, "Good night," to one another.

Giuseppe lay awake all night. *Angelina seemed genuine enough. Could I be blessed with another good woman? Had his wish on the bird come true? Please, Lord, I need a miracle. Don't look down on me. I can't wait a year to have a new mother for Sophia.* He sighed. *Would Angelina even consider me? I need to talk to Father Vincenzo.*

Angelina tossed to and fro, remembering what she had said to Giuseppe. *Was I too forward when I said I wanted a baby girl?* She was the only one, besides her former promised future husband, who knew what the doctor back home had told her: she was barren. As a result, her fiancé had released her from their betrothal. He wanted a large family. That was why Angelina was traveling to the New World. *Would she find someone, or would she remain a nanny the rest of her life?*

CHAPTER 26

INTEGRITY

There was a perfect calm on the sea the next morning. Giuseppe asked Father Vincenzo if he could eat breakfast with him and the Father readily agreed. He could sense that something important was on the fisherman's mind.

"Bless me, Father, for I have sinned," began Giuseppe. He continued on to explain that he did not want to dishonor his first wife in any way, but he had been admiring Angelina from afar. She was so gentle and caring with his daughter. Giuseppe asked if it was wrong to now want someone else to raise his daughter with him.

"You have not sinned," Father Vincenzo said gently, smiling at Giuseppe's sensitivity. "It is human nature to rear children with a partner, and it is going to be a rough life in the New World."

Giuseppe asked Father Vincenzo if he should make appropriate advances to Angelina. He was forthright and said he would not propose to Angelina unless he had the priest's approval. Vincenzo nodded and blessed him.

~ ~ ~

Giuseppe saw Angelina working diligently to prepare lunch with Giovanna, Cuncetta, and the other women. He slowly approached the line, hoping that Angelina would serve him. Unfortunately, it was Cuncetta who served him, but she was standing next to Angelina so he was able to ask her if she had been watching Sophia that morning. She told him that she had and that the baby was now napping.

"When can I see her?" he asked.

"After I finish distributing lunches," she replied. "Then I will bring Sophia to you."

After lunch, there was new vigor, higher morale, and greater hopefulness among the group, thanks to the shark capture. Antonino brought out his mandolin. Folks sang with enthusiasm. Somewhere in the middle of the celebration, Angelina brought Sophia to Giuseppe. The happy baby was handed to her father; then they joined in the singing. The sun shone brightly, and there was a warm, slight breeze, which was perfect for the relaxed gathering.

It was the first time Giuseppe had truly gazed into Angelina's eyes, and he noticed the deep warmth and kindness there. Giuseppe was nervous, but he nevertheless asked her if she had someone waiting for her in the New World.

"No," she said.

"Well then," he replied, "may I ask why you chose to leave home?"

She told him that she was very poor and had to work for four years to save enough money to travel to the New World. In America, she felt she would have a chance of finding a job and a suitable husband. Even though she knew it would be difficult at first, she felt she would no longer have to starve or struggle for money.

Giuseppe said he, too, wanted a better life. He explained that his wife had been unsure about the decision, but she had reluctantly agreed. Now that she was dead,

Giuseppe lamented his decision. He was now very worried about how he would be able to raise Sophia.

"I know you're good at taking care of babies," he continued, "and I know the other women can help when we get to the New World. Would you be able to help me care for Sophia?"

Angelina responded positively. She had grown very fond of Sophia over the past few weeks; though, of course, she could not share that she had also grown very fond of Giuseppe. He sighed with relief.

Dinnertime preparation was approaching, so Angelina had to excuse herself to help the others. *Was Giuseppe asking me to marry him or be a nanny?* she wondered. *If he wants me as a nanny, would he pay me? What would happen if he met a woman he* did *want to marry? How could I leave Sophia?* She tortured herself with one thought, *No man would want an infertile woman.*

Was Angelina agreeing to be Sophia's nanny, or saying she would marry me, Giuseppe wondered. *She was so beautiful and kind, surely she could find a better man than me. Oh, what a disgrace,* he thought. *What will people think of me, if I marry someone so soon?*

After dinner, Giuseppe went to bed, lying next to Sophia. She was making darling little cooing sounds, as though she were trying to tell him not to worry so much. She needed a caregiver, preferably a mother.

In the middle of the night, Sophia began to scream, and nothing Giuseppe did could get her to stop. He tried rocking her in his arms, but she continued to cry. He kissed her forehead and found she was burning up with fever.

He rushed out of the family area with Sophia. He lit a lantern, desperately searching for Angelina's space in the single women's area. After what felt like an eternity, he found Angelina. She was already awake, having heard the baby's cry. Giuseppe put the child in Angelina's arms, unsure of what else he could do. Angelina felt the heat radiating off the baby and instantly knew how sick she was. Her immediate instinct was to put Sophia in cool water. She asked Giuseppe to bring as many buckets of seawater as he could carry.

By now, a number of people were awake. Giovanna, half awake, wrestled to find rags in which to wrap Sophia. When the buckets were brought, the baby was repeatedly dipped into the water and then brought out quickly. This went on for several hours. At some point, Sophia began to violently vomit. Giuseppe called for Father Vincenzo, who came immediately. The captain soon followed him. He recognized the symptoms of scarlet fever. Sophia's skin was covered in a rash and it was starting to peel. After Father Vincenzo blessed them, Captain Scardino ordered Giuseppe, Sophia, and Angelina to be quarantined. He directed them to go below deck, under the sleeping area. They quickly cooperated. Sophia was cooler now, but still not cool enough. They would be quarantined for several days.

CHAPTER 27

DEVOTION

The Lord works in mysterious ways. On the third day, Sophia's temperature returned to normal. Neither Giuseppe nor Angelina had slept much during those days, but now they finally felt they would be able to rest some. The female passengers had been leaving food for the trio on the top stair during their quarantine.

In the intermittent, quieter moments, when Sophia was blessedly asleep, Angelina and Giuseppe talked. Giuseppe asked about Angelina's family, her childhood, her cooking specialties, her likes and dislikes. He began to realize that she was a special woman. She had such a nice laugh and sense of humor. His feelings for her were deepening; he detected that there was a sadness in her, but he did not know how to ask about it.

Angelina asked him about his life, family, education, and what he liked to eat. He told her that when he was a small boy, his father had taken him fishing on his boat. The boat was the only possession his parents had. Slowly, he had learned the fishing business from his father. He had known he was destined to become a fisherman like the other boys in his family. Baking he'd learned from the women in his family.

Angelina loved to listen to his fishing stories. She soon caught on, though, that some of his stories were exaggerated. In one of his favorite stories, he claimed that he had caught a six-foot long fish. She asked him if that was really true, and he just smiled, laughing when she jokingly frowned at his lack of response.

As the third day wore on, Giuseppe started to feel feverish and sick. Within an hour, his temperature spiked, and he began to vomit. Giuseppe had all the same symptoms as Sophia.

Angelina began using rags to cool him down. She called for more buckets of water. She soaked Giuseppe from head to toe over and over again. She asked her female friends on deck to have Father Vincenzo lead the passengers in prayer to heal him. Their prayers were loud enough to hear below deck. Angelina began to cry and pray, too. This man that she had grown so fond of could not die. Losing two loves at such a young age was inconceivable. She worked in a frenzy to cool him down. His skin began to peel as she soaked and cleaned him. After hours of continuous nursing, she collapsed and fell asleep.

After a few hours, she awoke to a hungry crying baby. Her women friends had again brought food to the top step. She masticated the food and fed it to Sophia. Then she checked Giuseppe. He had weathered the high temperature, and now he had stopped vomiting. He was shivering, so she lay across his chest to warm him. His temperature soon spiked again, and she spent the rest of the night soaking him. She began to feel as if this process of nursing and sickness would never end. When she was unable to continue, she again collapsed and fell asleep.

The fourth day came. Sophia and Giuseppe rested easily. Neither one was hot. Angelina yelled upstairs to let her friends know that they both were over the worst part of the illness and that their prayers had helped. Captain Scardino yelled back that because Giuseppe had fallen prey to the disease, they must continue to be quarantined for another two days. After feeding Sophia, Angelina fell into a deep slumber. When she awoke, it was the fifth day. Giuseppe was up, getting food from the top step. Even though he had been very sick, he could remember all the things Angelina had done for him and his daughter. Softly, he approached Angelina and bent down to feed her. She was ravenous.

She thanked him for helping her. While she was eating, he rocked and fed Sophia. He was still very pale and his skin was peeling, but he smiled widely. He put Sophia down to sleep. The two adults sat in silence for a few moments, gathering their thoughts. With all the confidence he could muster, Giuseppe asked Angelina to marry him. Shocked, she began to weep.

"Oh, Angelina," he said, panicking. "I didn't mean to make you cry. I wanted—I want—to make you happy."

After crying a while, Angelina spoke. "Giuseppe, before I can answer, you must know something about me."

What could it be? Was it too soon for her to love me? his thoughts flew.

She continued, "If this fact changes your mind to marry me, I will understand."

"What is it?" he asked.

She told him about her infertility and began to sob again. He came closer to her. Though he was shocked and a little disappointed because Italians love large families, he said it would be okay.

"We have Sophia to love, and I will have a son when she marries. You have shown us both so much love, I could not ask for a more devoted wife or a better mother for my daughter."

Angelina sobbed even harder.

CHAPTER 28

CRISIS

While the couple was quarantined, many things happened on deck. Captain Scardino saw a pod of whales and alerted the passengers. Daniele and Rosina were the first to rush to see the incredible sight. They laughed because they nearly knocked each other over. Daniele said she was a better dancer than a "pusher." With that, Rosina pushed and shoved him more.

After the whales passed, Placido organized teams to play cards. A number of passengers lined up. The game got intense, and everyone howled with laughter. Placido was watching closely to determine the winner. Antonino came in first.

"Since I came in first, that must be worth something."

"Yes," Placido said, "you deserve a kick in the pants," a sentiment that was put into action by several men. Even Giovanna attempted to kick him in jest. The crowd became uproarious.

"No, I'm sorry, Antonino," Placido said. "You're already our leader. You're not allowed to win at this too. Daniele, you followed the rules. You're the winner."

Daniele threw his cane in the air and grabbed Rosina into a hug without thinking. Placido told them that the prize was that Rosina and Daniele could be first in the dinner line.

Daniele was now very adept with the wooden leg and cane Paolo had carved for him. He was feeling so comfortable with Rosina that he no longer felt awkward or embarrassed because of his limitations. Rosina accepted him for who he was, a strong, independent man who knew what he wanted out of life. He had been trained as a doctor. His dream was a romantic Italian woman for his wife and a "boatload of children." There was no question that Rosina was his idea of a perfect wife.

After dinner together, Daniele and Rosina found a quiet place to talk. He professed his love for her and told her that he wanted to spend the rest of his life with her. Rosina gasped for air. She had known this day would eventually come.

"I can't discuss this now," she told him sadly.

"Why not?" he asked, shocked.

"I just can't."

"Do you love me?"

"Yes, of course," Rosina replied.

"Then why can't we discuss it now? Do I need to ask your father's permission first?"

"That would be the traditional way of handling it," she admitted.

"Then may I write the letter now and have Captain Scardino deliver it after his return voyage?"

"No," she said, clearly tormented. "I can't discuss this now, and I may never be able to discuss it."

With that statement, she fled from him, tears rolling down her cheeks. *Oh dear, where is Father Vincenzo? Not up here. Oh dear. Well, I shouldn't trouble him now. The morning. Yes, the morning will be better.*

Where can I begin? How much should I tell? If I do not tell Father the whole story, how can he give me advice? Can I? Should I?

There had not been a question in her mind before this voyage. Now everything was mixed up. She prayed determinedly to request help from the almighty father. She became so nervous that she fainted. One of her friends found her and called for help. The first mate rushed over as she was conscious.

"Do you need a doctor?" he asked Rosina. "Should we get Daniele?"

"No," she said. "Not Daniele. Call Father Vincenzo."

Even though it was late, he rushed to Rosina's side. He was afraid that she, too, had contracted scarlet fever, but she was not feverish.

"How can I help you?" he asked.

She told Father that she needed privacy to tell him what was on her mind. They went to the far side of the bow and settled themselves as comfortably as they could. Then she explained her predicament to the priest.

"Father, my papa is a mafia boss. When I was a small child, Papa wanted to stop the war with a neighboring mafia clan. As a result, I was promised to the other family as a wife for their oldest son, Giacomo. The son is fifty years my senior. His wife died during the birth of their ninth child."

"My dear mamma helped me to save money for this trip. She could not let me marry such an evil man. My father will think I joined a cloistered convent because that is what I wrote in my last note. I wanted to escape from everyone who would make me honor this promise. I do not want any part of the mafia life. I would rather commit suicide."

"You need never say that again," Father Vincenzo

replied. "You know that you would burn in hell for all eternity."

"Yes, Father, I know. I'm sorry. But what can I do? I'm desperate. I love Daniele dearly and I know that I would have a blessed life with him. He asked me to marry him tonight."

"How did you respond?"

"I said that I could not discuss it then . . . or possibly ever."

"How did he react?"

"He was very confused. He asked if he needed to write a letter to my papa asking permission to marry me."

"You love Daniele and want to live a normal life with him, but you want to remain incognito so that no one will find you?"

"Yes, Father."

"What will become of your family if your parents cannot facilitate the wedding? Will that result in a bloody war again?"

"I can't think that," she said. "I can't be responsible for that."

Father Vincenzo reminded her of the first commandment. "'Thou shalt honor thy father and mother,'" he recited. "You are being excessively bold with your proposition. Sicilian women listen to their fathers."

"Father," she replied, "Yes, I've broken with tradition, but I haven't dishonored my mother. I did what she said to do. Is it possible to confess half a sin?"

Father had to laugh. Rosina was so sprightly and determined.

"What about your sin, lying to your father?" he asked.

"I confess that to you, too," Rosina said.

"Well," the Father responded, "I agree with you that living with an evil man would cause you to sin, in that respect. Your secret is safe with me, Rosina. Now, go and tell Daniele the truth."

CHAPTER 29

JOYFULNESS

That same night, Antonino and Giovanna were relaxing on the top deck, viewing the beautiful ocean waves and feeling the gentle rocking of the ship. Antonino asked Giovanna if he could "Americanize" her name to Vanna. In return, Vanna asked Antonino if she could call him Nino. They both liked their new nicknames.

Neither one could resist speaking about Italy. "I worry so much about our families in Sicily," Nino began. "My father had to contend with attacks from the Cosca family so often. But it will take even more deaths to end this vendetta. My mother helps Papa as much as she can, but she has many responsibilities. Papa taught her how to shoot a revolver and a rifle."

He could remember the war between the families even from when he was a child.

"My family never attacked the Cosca family," he continued. "But Papa always had to be on high alert, because he never knew when they would attack."

Vanna's family had experienced the same thing when she was growing up. The Carlucci family was enemies with her family because they were jealous of their wealth from the salt fields.

"Remember when both our families joined together to meet with the Coscas and the Carluccis?" she asked.

Both Vanna's father, Alessandro, and Nino's father, Francesco, had agreed that they would meet with the two families to reach a settlement. The other families wanted money and part ownership of the sulfur and salt mines. It took multiple meetings to work through the issues, but agreements were eventually reached.

"I miss them all so much already," Vanna lamented.

"So do I," Nino agreed.

"Our families will forever be in our hearts and prayers," she said.

Meanwhile, Rosina searched for Daniele. She found him reading a book on deck. She called his name, but he did not respond. *Perhaps he does not hear me.* She called him again. Instead of reading the book, Daniele was merely looking at the pages, thinking of her. Hearing her call, he looked up at her. His eyes were so sad.

"Daniele, I have so much to tell you." As she detailed the truth about her life circumstances, Daniele's demeanor changed from sadness to shock to horror and then, finally, to joy. After she had finished telling him everything, she collapsed into his arms, hugging him tightly. She asked if he still wanted to marry her.

"Yes, of course!" he shouted. "Let's ask Father Vincenzo to perform the ceremony tomorrow!" Rosina beamed. She readily agreed.

That afternoon, they announced the news first to Father Vincenzo and then to Antonino. Per Nino's request, the captain rang the bell to gather all the passengers so they could announce their plan. When they heard, the group cheered and began to sing and dance. A group of people went to the stairs and yelled below to announce the good news to Giuseppe and Angelina, who were still quarantined until the next day. When they heard the news, Giuseppe looked questioningly at Angelina. She could guess his thoughts.

"Why don't we ask Father to perform a double ceremony?" Giuseppe asked her. "If Daniele and Rosina don't mind, that is."

Rosina laughed heartily. "Are you serious?" she asked.

Giuseppe yelled to get their friends' attention. There was so much happening on deck that they could not hear him. He tried a number of times. Frustrated, Giuseppe began to climb the stairs. Angelina tried to stop him because they had one more day left of their quarantine, but Giuseppe continued on his mission. At the top of the stairs, he yelled as loudly as he could and was heard at last. He retreated down the stairs. People came running. Giuseppe asked to speak with Daniele and Rosina. They promptly came to the top of the staircase.

"Hello down there!" Daniele called.

Giuseppe extended a happy congratulatory message to them.

They thanked him.

Continuing, Giuseppe told them that he had a serious idea that he wanted to share.

"Go on, but speak louder," Daniele said.

"Do you mind if Angelina and I marry in a double ceremony with you and Rosina tomorrow?"

The crowd cheered even louder when they heard Giuseppe's idea. Daniele and Rosina looked at each other with great surprise. Rosina nodded her head and Daniele yelled back his agreement.

"Yes, let's do it! Everyone should be this happy!"

Everyone cheered, even Captain Scardino. The women began assembling cloth crowns with streamers for the brides. Rosina started sewing to finish the wedding dress they had found in the pirates' chest. She had first asked if Angelina wanted to wear it, but she had insisted that Rosina wear it. She had her mother's dress.

Rosina asked Angelina if she would like "*La Serenata*" ("Serenade") that evening before bedtime.

"Oh, yes," Angelina said. "I love that tradition the night before the wedding. It is so romantic."

The ladies asked their soon-to-be spouses if that could be arranged. The two men immediately went to Nino and Placido to see if they were willing to help serenade their brides.

Traditionally, the serenade was sung by a future husband under the window of his wife-to-be the night before the ceremony.

Nino said they would sing with the grooms when the sun was setting that evening.

Later that day, Antonino and Vincenzo led the men in positioning the fishing net.

"We want a real celebration with good food and wine for the weddings," Nino said.

Eventually, they caught a number of smaller fish. Some of the women began making macaroni and garlic bread. There would not be a lot of food left after the ceremonies, but they knew they were getting close to their destination, and they were so jubilant about the couples, it did not seem to matter. The Lord would provide, they knew.

The sunset was beautiful that evening. Nino, Placido, Daniele, and Giuseppe sat on the deck and began to play and sing amorous Sicilian songs for about an hour. The women were so happy and the men were gratified to be able to perform the ladies' request.

CHAPTER 30

CELEBRATION

"Remember me when you wear it," she said. "I'll always love you and pray for you. May God bless you in abundance during your life. I'll always be with you in spirit. When you have your first child," she had said, laughing, "you'll know how I felt when I first saw your wrinkled, red face and your big mouth screaming." Rosina had laughed with her. "Motherhood is magical. There are no words to describe the feeling of becoming a mother."

Her mother's face had then fallen. "I must tell you the truth about your papa," she continued seriously. "He didn't want to be a Mafia Boss. Your grandfather named him as his successor. Grandpa had only two sons, but he had many daughters. His oldest son died of consumption at fifteen. That left your father to carry on the business. Your father initially refused, but he was whipped until he agreed.

"Personally, I didn't know this until you were eight years old. That's when your father thought he could end the bloodshed between the families. He thought by offering you as a wife to Giacomo, the oldest son in the Vonzano family, he could create a truce.

"Your father thought he was doing the right thing; he thought our family would then be protected. He truly believed this would be the best solution for everyone. Your papa loves you very much. He didn't think you would be hurt by this agreement.

"The Vonzano family promised they would stop the feud when you married Giacomo. Papa thought you'd live a rich life with everything you had ever wanted. Now that you're seventeen, they're planning a wedding. That is why you must leave. We can no longer trust their promises."

Her mother reached into her pocket and drew out a small package. She handed it to Rosina. "Here is enough money for the cruise to America. You will be free from all the madness here."

"Mamma," Rosina said with tears in her eyes, "I love you so much. I'm afraid. I've heard stories about the journey to America and about life there."

"I'm sorry, Rosina, but it is the only way to protect you from that evil family and from Giacomo."

"I understand, Mamma." With that exclamation, she had thrown her arms around her mother and sobbed. "I'll miss you so much."

"If there is a way to get word to you, I will," her mother had promised. "Now hurry, my precious darling, or you'll miss the boat. Your father is visiting his mother. You'll be safe under the guise of night. Put this hooded coat on and keep your face toward the ground. No one will know the plan if you go now."

Rosina clutched the heirloom locket, fondly remembering what her mamma had said. *I wish she could be here with me now, on my wedding day*, she thought. *I didn't expect it to come so soon.*

Now that she knew the truth about her father, Rosina wished he were there to give her away. She realized she might never see her mamma or papa again. Her heart sank.

I must be strong now for my husband and for my future family, she thought. For a moment, she felt overwhelmed. She needed to focus on having a blessed life with a good man.

Meanwhile, Angelina was preparing, too. She pulled her hair back with a bow and pinched her cheeks to add color to her face. *Thank you, Dear Lord, for giving me a special man that I can love,* she thought. *I never really expected it, but I earnestly prayed for it.*

Angelina's mamma had worn flowers in her hair that Papa had given her. He had told her she was the most beautiful woman in the world. They had been so in love that nothing else had mattered to them other than spending the rest of their lives together.

Both brides ascended from the stairs to meet Father at the aft of the ship. The crowd loudly cheered for them. Their soon-to-be husbands smiled radiantly as they saw their loves. Antonino and Placido gave the brides away. The six of them solemnly walked toward Father Vincenzo. The grooms faced the escorts as they handed each bride to her partner. Women cried with joy. Young widows reflected on their wedding day with tears welling in their eyes and the pain in their throats prevented them from praying out loud with the others. The sun cast a gorgeous orange tint on this hopeful group. All knew that their future lives would be drastically different, but they felt assured that God was leading their journey.

Antonino hushed the congregation. Father Vincenzo opened his Bible and donned his crucifix. He read inspiring passages. A group of thoughtful female passengers had crocheted two large rosaries. They were so big that they were lassoed around each couple's shoulders. It symbolized the joining together of the brides and grooms in God's name. It was a special tradition that added elegance to the gathering. Later, the rosaries would be heirlooms for their children.

The Mass and the ceremony that followed were beautiful. The audience offered up their communion for the married couples, wishing them fruitful lives. Those who were already married clutched their children and renewed their vows together with the bridal group. Those who were single linked their arms or held hands. The ritual was finalized and the grooms were allowed to kiss their brides.

Nino held Vanna firmly by the hand during the ceremony. He had a way of signaling her with three hand squeezes when they were around other people. He was saying, "I love you." Vanna squeezed his hand four times as a response. It meant, "I love you more."

~ ~ ~

The brides and grooms led the parade with lit candles around the deck three times for luck under the dusky sky. Everyone followed them, laughing, to the beat of the captain's drum. When the parade concluded, wine was served. Nunzio and Cuncetta, along with other volunteers, had cooked the meal.

The fish was delicately seasoned and the pasta had garlic, onions, and olive oil in it. For dessert, Nunzio and Cuncetta had made orzo pudding from goat's milk because they did not have the right ingredients to make a cake. The crowd clapped and cheered at the dessert. Nunzio and Cuncetta playfully took a bow.

After dessert, it was time for the music. Antonino grabbed his mandolin and Placido prepared his squeeze-box. Antonino took a few practice strums and cleared his throat. The duo wanted to play romantic songs first. The brides and grooms danced during the first song. They were gazing into each other's eyes as they moved clumsily around the unsteady deck, due to the active waves. The group applauded after the first song.

Many had enjoyed the wine and were anxious to dance themselves. After a few slow songs, the crowd began requesting traditional fast songs. They formed a dance line and broke off into groups for the tarantella. Other popular dances were the *ballo* (changes tempo and meter), *pizzica* (like tarantella), *passamezzo* (1 or 2 chord progressions), and *saltarello* (leaping steps). All were lively dances with both partnered and solo rhythmic moves. The dancing lasted far into the night. Daniele was determined to function normally, even with a cane, and that included dance steps.

Eventually people began to retreat below deck for sleep. There came an awkward moment when the brides and grooms did not know where to sleep. Unbeknown to them, their friends had created two little "nests" for the couples. They had strung up makeshift curtains so that the two couples could have a little privacy. One "nest" was in Angelina's typical area and one was organized in Giuseppe's and Sophia's area.

Morning came faster than most wanted. The crew was up early the next morning, but the passengers were far slower than usual to get on deck. Antonino, however, was in deep meditation that morning, huddled in a secluded area on deck. He held his private life close to his chest.

He was daydreaming of Sicily, *pezzo di cielo*. Nino had promised to protect Father Vincenzo and to help him build a basilica in America; that had to be his first priority. But Giovanna knew she would never be a second priority for him and he knew he would never be a second priority for her. They were a team and this was their mission, literally.

CHAPTER 31

HELPFULNESS

Vincenzo and Daniele had questions. Antonino said there would be a group who would be the welcoming committee in New Orleans with temporary housing until they could make other arrangements. Placido, Rosina, Paulo, Cuncetta, Giuseppe, Angelina, and Nunzio were also solicited for that evening's meeting after dinner. The agenda was clear: figuring out a way to mobilize people in an orderly way so that they could build a functioning, worthy Catholic community.

Antonino opened the meeting, explaining what they needed to accomplish before landing in New Orleans.

"Once we reach Louisiana," he began, "there will be a 'welcoming committee' to meet us. They will provide free room and board for us if we work for them. That will only be until we leave for west of DeRidder. In that sense, anyway, our immediate needs will be met.

"Our mission for now is to plan how we will organize ourselves, so we can build our new community. We think we have the land already, with the deed from the pirate's chest, so we hope that will be our home. We have all been trained in a trade. Let's see if we can formulate a plan. I invite Father Vincenzo to be our first contributor."

"Thank you, Antonino. I would like to nominate you as the town's mayor. You have been trained in leadership, math, and engineering, along with so many other skills taught at the university. You are our pillar of light and inspiration."

The group clapped loudly. Nino accepted the honor.

"I would also like to be the town's cobbler," he added, "just as my father taught me to be. Many of us need shoes."

The priest nodded and continued. He related how he and Antonino had been commissioned by Popes Leo XIII and Pius X and Cardinal Cusimano to build their church in the New World, adding that Giovanna and Daniele had been instructed to help them organize the church's construction and community building. He explained that the first building the group erected would have to be their wooden church, which would serve as their worship space until the grand masonry basilica was completed. The dome, arches, friezes, double colonnades, a semicircular apse, rotunda, and stained-glass windows planned for the building would keep craftsmen employed for years. The vaulted ceilings would be twenty feet high, domed, and covered with paintings, similar to the Sistine Chapel. An elaborate altar would be situated under the first dome. The archangels would be gorgeous. White billowy clouds and a light blue sky, complete with gold leaf accents, would make up the backdrop for the Trinity, with the blessed Mother and Joseph standing alongside.

The community members would live in tents outside the covered wagons, until the wooden church was built, and then they could start on housing.

Paolo stepped forward next. He was trained as a carpenter and he volunteered to help build the church. Antonino asked him how he thought the construction should be organized.

"I know some men on the ship have carpentry experience," he replied. "If the group agrees, I could organize those men and begin training them, even while we're still on the ship. That way, once we reach the land, we'll be able to start construction right away."

The group readily agreed.

"Who else has some thoughts to share?" Antonino asked.

"Cuncetta and I have a dream," Nunzio said, "to open a restaurant. We can teach some people how to garden, hunt, butcher, and cook." He shared that Nino had given him the butchering tools and a gun found in one of the pirates' chests. "A few have already begun volunteering to help with the food." Nunzio's group would cook the fresh food for everyone while homes were being built. The response was met with passionate shouts of joy. Giuseppe added that he was a baker and fisherman by trade, and he would enjoy teaching others what skills they needed.

Angelina divulged that she had been a nanny in the old country. "I will train the women and girls who do not know how to care for children. That way, while mothers are involved with other tasks, we can tend to the babies and children. Then, everyone can be productive."

Giuseppe hugged her. He was so proud of her.

"I will start a school," said Giovanna. "Our 'deck school' has been successful. Everyone who has attended has learned to read, and they've also developed an appreciation of science, art, math, and drawing."

An excited whoop was heard among the passengers. By now, others had begun listening to what was being said.

Rosina said she could sew and nurse the sick with Daniele, a *dottore*. She knew how to make clothing for children and adults, and she could also make tablecloths, curtains, night wear, underwear, hats, gloves, coats, and just about anything else that was needed. Rosina replied that she would be delighted to accommodate them after she had finished making all the vestments and altar cloths that Father Vincenzo would need.

Nino had facilitated the meeting and now was able to summarize what everyone had said. Giovanna wrote it all down.

The crowd was feeling the power of camaraderie and everyone was infused with a sense of purpose. In a new land, it could never be every man for himself. With their group, it didn't have to be.

"I believe you all will be the leaders of our newly formed community," Nino said. "Our group will not succeed without each and every person's special skills and talents. I believe we agreed that recruiting others and training them will begin tomorrow, is that correct?"

Everyone responded in the affirmative energetically and forcefully. Figuring out how they would go about their responsibilities would be a continual process. The talents of the group were bringing them far.

CHAPTER 32

HOPE

Many people milled around on the deck the next morning. The passengers could feel that something exciting was happening. Antonino used the captain's bell to get everyone's attention. He summarized what the leaders were going to be doing: recruiting for new volunteers and mobilizing passengers interested in the various trades or skills they had to offer their new town. He explained that the training would commence immediately. He requested that if anyone else had skills to please come forward, so they could help them organize too.

In support of Nino, Vincenzo announced that the leadership group had met and planned this process, enabling them to start their town successfully. He also informed everyone that Nino would be their mayor. Each occupation leader found a significant number of people who were interested in their particular area. Their daily schedule would be to teach or train from sunrise to sunset until they reached New Orleans. Everyone was determined to be useful and complaints about the long hours were minimal.

Antonino called a meeting with the leaders three days after the process had begun, to ask for a progress report. Daniele remarked that their process had gone smoothly, mostly due to everyone's cooperative attitude.

"You know," Daniele said, "it's incredible to have this feeling of responsible empowerment. It was never like this back home. The Mafia would force people to do things they didn't want to do and people would comply out of fear for their own lives or the well-being of their families. Let's vow to never let the Mafia rule us again."

The group, unsurprisingly, sincerely supported Daniele's proposition.

Antonino reflected on his position as the mayor. "It's ahead of its time, but we will have to give it grave consideration. We need to plan what we're going to do if the mafia tries to take control."

When Sunday came, the passengers rested and played cards after Mass. People laughed and joked, and there was a lightheartedness all around. The group knew its journey was going to end soon. Wine was passed around. The travelers were hopeful. What sacrifices they had made on this trip had been worth risking, and they knew, through their dedication and hard work, they would have a fortunate future.

Placido and Antonino started to play their instruments. Even the captain's first mate had a sailor beat the drum. It did not take long for the passengers to start dancing. The rhythm of the ship swayed back and forth, with the ebb and flow of the sea. There was a slightly salty wind breathing fresh air in their direction. It was a welcome relief from the stagnant air below deck.

They were desperate to go to America to leave behind the squalor they had experienced in Palermo. Even if they had known ahead of time the conditions in which they would be housed on the ship, they still would have opted to go. These people were desperate to escape the mafia, the conflicts, the poor living conditions, the hunger, the hope-lessness, and the helplessness.

On Monday morning, everyone's training began promptly at sunrise. Vincenzo had invited some women to train with him. They would be in charge of the altar and finding flowers to decorate various areas of the church. They would also be responsible for cleaning the altar cloths, all the vestments, and the church. The ladies promised that if there was anything else he needed, they would handle it in a timely fashion.

Meanwhile, a man with a serious expression approached Nino. He introduced himself as Doctor Maximiliano Fortunati from Messina, Sicily.

"You might remember me from the university," he said.

He was right. He and Antonino had passed each other in the corridors a number of times. Fortunati was unforgettable at six feet tall. During tough times, one didn't see many people who weighed four hundred pounds.

"Of course," Antonino said. "I always wondered who you were. I assumed that you were a professor or researcher." Nino was a little shocked he had not seen him on the ship before that day. "How have I missed you?" he asked Maximiliano. "We have been sailing for quite some time."

Maximiliano explained that he had been recuperating from the flu. He had traveled on this ship, rather than waiting for the April tour, because his mother had been ailing in Louisiana and he wanted to see her as soon as he could. He had spoken to the captain and was aware of what Antonino was trying to accomplish with everyone's training. Maximiliano volunteered to help the group however he could.

"Where will your group be settling?" he asked.

"We will be traveling to acreage near the Calcasieu River," Antonino responded, "in northwestern Louisiana."

"Well," Maximiliano said, "my mother is in the central part of Louisiana."

Nino showed him the land deed and map he had gotten from the pirates' ship. Maximiliano studied it carefully. "I don't think she is far from your destination," he said after a few moments of deep concentration.

"We can discuss this later, but right now the training is occurring," Nino said. "It would be best if you worked with Daniele and his group. Daniele is also a doctor, and Rosina, his wife, is a nurse and a midwife. They would enjoy knowing that we have another doctor in our midst. Their group is on the aft deck. Thank you again for your help."

Antonino watched as the clouds grew angrier. The captain rang his bell to warn passengers to go below deck. Heavy rain soon followed. The wind was challenging the rain to a forceful duel.

The onset of the rain was so extreme that in little time, steerage contained a pool of water. Captain Scardino ordered his men to get the "honey pots." He had the stronger men form a line on the stairs to bail the water. As the rain fell faster, the men sped up their pace, trying to compete with the elements.

Back and forth, up and down, and in a circuitous fashion the ship whirled. Volunteers had difficulty holding on to the railing and bailing water at the same time. The first mate and his men attempted to take down the sails. In the steam engine room, the men stopped stoking wood. If the ship fought back too strongly, it would capsize.

It was Christmas Eve, 1905. Vanna said to the men, "Just think, a year ago, we were spending Christmas at the Vatican!"

If not here, people would have been home with their families singing, playing music, dancing, or watching the children perform the pageantry of the birth of Jesus Christ. Father Vincenzo led the nervous travelers in prayer. No one slept that night.

CHAPTER 33

MYSTERIOUS MAN

The storm was still active on Christmas morning and many passengers were seasick. Father Vincenzo conducted confessions for those who were afraid this would be their last day on earth. Wailing and crying permeated the ship. Ladies had their rosaries out, and many kissed their crosses as they prayed. Antonino tried to deliver some encouraging words, but even he felt they might be defeated. There had been significant wear and tear on the vessel and the people.

As noon neared, the buckets of water had to be dumped less frequently, and people became seasick less often. Finally, steerage was cleared of water.

"Perhaps God sent the rains to purge some of the wretched odors in steerage," Father Vincenzo said. Even though steerage still had some foul scents, it was much better than before the storm. With all the water gushing onto the ship, there were plenty of fish on deck to cook for dinner. Vincenzo noted that God worked the strangest miracles.

Slowly, people began to emerge from below deck. They wanted to smell the food and fresh air again and to dry out their clothes. Frowns soon turned into grateful smiles. They thanked the captain and his men, not forgetting to also thank Father Vincenzo and Antonino. Giuseppe gathered the fish on deck so that Nunzio,

Cuncetta, and the rest of their group could fix a culinary surprise. Nunzio and Cuncetta's group poached the fish in white wine and lemon. They added salt, pepper, oregano, thyme, and basil.

The delicious aroma permeated the ship, disguising the despicable odors. The last of the macaroni was brought up to be cooked. Goat cheese, vegetables, and olive oil were melted into the pasta for a rare treat. Before they began eating, everyone knelt to have Father Vincenzo lead them in a prayer thanking God for the birth of their Lord and for their salvation. Father added a beautiful prayer of gratitude for saving their wooden home and everyone in it. This Christmas would never be forgotten.

After dinner, Captain Scardino approached Nino.

"How are you doing today?" the captain asked.

"Much better than the last two days," Nino replied. "Your sailing crew did a remarkable job keeping the ship afloat. I've never experienced such a storm. I guess it's to be expected on the open seas this time of year."

"Yes," Scardino said. "Our patron saints of Sicily, *Santo Leoluca, Santa Rosalia, and Santo Bernardo,* were watching over us."

"We definitely have a destiny to fulfill," Antonino proclaimed.

The captain appeared to have something on his mind other than the weather. He began, "I saw you speaking with Doctor Maximiliano Fortunati."

"Yes," replied Antonino, "I was quite astonished that I hadn't seen him on the ship before now. He said you'd let him sleep in first class and that he'd been ill for some time.

I recommended he introduce himself to Daniele, Rosina, and the rest of the medical group."

The captain shuffled his feet a little, as if it were difficult beginning what he had to say. "Antonino, he must not know that I have spoken to you."

"Why?"

Captain Scardino stuttered slightly when he said, "I have doubts about the *dottore*."

"What do you mean?"

"The doctor is a very powerful man. I can't say anything more," Scardino said. "I have to tend to the ship now."

Nino was perplexed. Nino and Vanna requested a meeting with Vincenzo and Daniele. Placido went to find them and send them up. When they approached, Vincenzo was inquisitive, and Daniele had a skip in his step.

"On a serious note," Nino began, "I want to share with you the conversation I just had with the captain. There is a man on board staying in first class."

"Really?" Vincenzo said. "We thought there were no first-class passengers."

Antonino motioned them over to where they could see first class but not be seen and lowered his voice.

"The captain said that he'd seen me speaking to him but didn't say much. The stranger introduced himself as Doctor Maximiliano Fortunati, from Messina, Sicily. I had seen him a few times at the university. Vincenzo, you may recognize him, too, if he emerges from the cabin again. The impression I got from the captain was that the doctor is a very powerful man and should be watched."

"Why should we care about him?" Daniele asked.

"For now, I don't know," said Nino, "but I thought you should be aware of what the captain said."

"Yes, thanks for telling us," Vincenzo said. "What do you want us to do?"

"Just watch him for now, if you see him. He's about six feet tall, has one elongated eyebrow and is large around the waist. He wears a green copula hat, has a thick mustache, and smokes Toscano cigars. In fact, here he comes now, out of the cabin."

CHAPTER 34

SUSPICIONS

The four friends observed that four men were meeting with the doctor. Max waved the unknown men over to enter his quarters. The men turned around to see if anyone was watching them before entering. The four leaders continued their conversation, as though they were not paying any attention.

Daniele, who was an excellent artist, offered to draw a portrait of the men. He drew them quickly, in about fifteen minutes, so he wouldn't forget their faces. The group then waited until the fifth man came out of the cabin. He finally emerged, several minutes later. They heard loud, angry voices. Then, Maximiliano spoke, and the four men immediately stopped their quarrel. The men seemed to be afraid of him.

Daniele began to draw the last man. They were speaking in Italian. One man was young, about seventeen or eighteen years old, and his clothes were filthy. He had no shoes. Another man had long, sandy-colored hair that was tied back with a red bandana. His face was badly scarred from a fire. The next man was very short, bald, and looked much older than the other two. He wore a black-and-white plaid shirt that had a large tear on the left pocket. Even though he was bald, he had a full black beard and a handlebar mustache. The fourth individual was like no other man aboard the ship. He walked with a heavy limp and wore an eye patch. He was dark skinned and highly wrinkled. Daniele had captured every detail. The drawings were to be shared with other trusted passengers so that they could identify these men, in case of trouble.

Vincenzo said he did not like what he had observed. Daniele agreed, but Giovanna believed that they were innocent until they found them guilty. Just as the men were concluding their meeting, Daniele asked if Nino or Vincenzo had checked where their money was hidden, because he had not checked for a while. They looked at each other with horror on their faces. They had not inspected it since before the storm started the day before. They decided that if they found the treasure to be missing, they would immediately climb to the deck and decide what to do next.

They went to steerage together. Attempting to look unconcerned, the foursome walked down the stairs. Antonino held his breath. Vincenzo prayed, and Daniele panted with fear. Giovanna was very serious, and her brows were wrinkled. There were many people in steerage, so they had to work slyly, hoping they would not be conspicuous. They sat down in a circle and crossed their legs, pretending to be holding a conversation. As they spoke, Nino slowly felt for the box under their belongings. He opened the box while staring into Giovanna's eyes.

"I'll look first," Nino said with a shaking voice. He slowly looked down into the box. "*Santa Maria!*" (Saint Mary! The expression meant "Oh no!").

The money was gone. With trembling hands, he returned the box to the "safe" place where it had been. The group ascended the stairs, so they could formulate a plan to recover their valuables. They exchanged vacant looks of disbelief when they reached the deck. Before anyone could speak, the captain joined their group.

"What's happening? You look as though you have all seen the devil!"

"We've been robbed," Father Vincenzo said with vengeance in his voice. "There must be retribution. The papal money was stolen and much of it was meant to build our new church. We can't disappoint God."

The captain was speechless. When he regained his composure, he wanted to know if they knew who had taken the treasure.

"We think four men are in collusion with Fortunati," Nino said. "When you were telling me about Max, I felt you were warning me about him. Am I right?"

"Yes," the captain responded slowly. "The truth of the matter is that he is part of the *'Cosa Nostra'* (Our Thing) Mafia, but I am not supposed to know that and could be killed if he finds out I revealed it."

The friends listened intently.

The captain continued. "He is sleeping in first class because he commandeered it, even though he hasn't paid for it. Max, also known by his mafia nickname, 'Mad Dog,' threatened my family if I did not provide five first-class rooms for his men, who are his soldiers. They are just a few of his gang; there are many more back in Sicily."

"What can we do to get our valuables back?" Daniele asked.

"We can't allow them to disembark, or we will never find the treasure," replied Nino.

"If you plan to get it back," the captain said, "let me know when. Under other circumstances, I wouldn't get involved, but you are all my dear friends now." With that, he departed.

Daniele was the first to speak. "We need more than the four of us to solve this. Who can we trust with this plan? No doubt we can trust Paulo, Cuncetta, Giuseppe, Angelina, Nunzio, Placido, and the crew."

The rest agreed. Daniele and Nunzio had guns if they needed them.

"The light is almost gone. Let's start planning this first thing in the morning," Antonino advised. They said good night to one another, all worrying about what horrendous thing they might have to do.

CHAPTER 35

MUTINY

As the sun rose December 30, guns exploded. People awoke in a panic. Many ran up to the deck to see what was happening. The captain, first mate, and the crew, minus one who steered the ship, were tied up and gagged. Max and his four men had rifles and were holding the captives at gunpoint.

The captain strained to turn his face toward Nino. He looked helpless and defeated. The criminals pushed Cuncetta around to coerce her into making breakfast. Nunzio stayed close to her. The cooks asked the apprentices to help them. Breakfast was cheese frittata, garlic toast, and goat's milk. The women were allowed to feed the prisoners with the robbers watching them closely to ensure the captives were not untied.

After breakfast, the planners agreed to meet in steerage. "This is a travesty," began Nino, with rage in his voice. "Last night I had several ideas in mind for how we could recover our treasure. Whatever plan we agree on, their guns must be confiscated first."

One idea was to threaten Maximiliano with a gun when he's alone, so he'd reveal where they are hiding the treasure. Another was to get the strongest men to tie up Max's men using brute force. The third plan was to force them to walk the plank, after they'd revealed where they'd stashed the money.

Nino paused to ask Vincenzo if the last plan would be approved by God. Vincenzo reminded him that they would have to confess their actions. Daniele said he thought they should agree to do the first two ideas. Vincenzo agreed. They would need the element of surprise and to go after them all at once.

"Let's spread out and reveal our plan to the people we agreed were trustworthy," added Placido. They completed their task as quickly as they could and then retired to bed. The next morning, before the sun rose, the hooligans would be captured. They would need to be gagged, too. It had become the group's New Year's resolution to be rid of the interlopers.

Antonino quietly organized the team, which had grown significantly, before the first rays of dawn. Daniele stood at the top of the stairs to watch for the sun's ascent. On this morning, the sun was covered with clouds; it had begun to rain during the night.

No one had worn shoes so that they would stay silent. Daniele even muffled the sound of his leg and cane. Nino was the first to reach the deck. He could hear the trouble-makers snoring. Cautiously, the leaders surrounded the group and got ropes ready in their hands. Some had knives, in case there was a fight. Giovanna had organized the "Pots and Pans Brigade." The team crept toward the first-class quarters.

Antonino silently opened Fortunati's door and found him sleeping on his stomach. *Perfect!*

Nino hit Maximiliano on the head with his gun. Giovanna followed with her skillet and grabbed Max's gun.

Then, the four of them tied his feet and arms and gagged him. There was no way he could yell for help now or escape.

As the other groups struggled to bind and gag their criminals, women followed Gio's template. They clocked the mutineers. Two of the four men were now bound and gagged. The other two were still fighting.

Suddenly, another gunshot was heard. The youngest of the four mutineers fell to the floor. His gun had accidentally gone off in the struggle and mortally wounded him. The last of the four continued fighting, but he was greatly outnumbered. It was not long before he was overpowered and tied up. The ship was finally resecured. The captain and his crew were unbound. Guards stood outside each first-class cabin.

The passengers cheered so loudly that they joked that their family in Sicily could hear them. There was something symbolic about their victory on New Year's Eve. Tomorrow they could begin the year with a clean slate.

The women wrapped the dead brigand in a tablecloth and Father Vincenzo performed a funeral service for him. The young fellow was tossed into the sea with a prayer that God might save his soul. If sharks might take his body, well, that was up to nature. Perhaps they could capture another for dinner.

Captain Scardino was elated that Antonino and his gallant group had defended the crew and the ship. He was going to share with all who would listen what heroes they were. Many passengers lifted Nino and his team onto their shoulders and paraded them around the deck to illustrate their gratitude for their courage. The first mate began to play the drum and singing soon followed. As soon as the crowd let the heroes down, Nino and Placido played their instruments, and then the dancing began.

~ ~ ~

The captain and first officer offered to help the men with interrogating the invaders. That way, it would seem more official. They began their interrogation with the violator who they perceived as the weakest: the short, bald man. Paolo and Placido brought the first violator into the captain's quarters. They threw him on the floor and held him down with their feet.

Captain Scardino began. "You are disgusting," he shouted. "Insane! Mutiny—on my ship! Stealing from my passengers! Insane!"

Antonino had never observed the bellicose side of the captain, nor the combative part of the first mate. They kicked the prisoner, then pulled him up to a chair. The prisoner tried to look stoic.

They played their roles well. If the heroes had not been friends with the captain and his first officer, they would have been afraid of them.

"On my ship!" he bellowed. "No, *not* on my ship!" He got right in the prisoner's gagged face, so he was close enough to spit on him.

"Where's the money?"

The captive said nothing. They removed the gag.

"Let's try again. Where's the money?"

The first mate slugged the prisoner in the stomach. The man remained quiet. This process went on for an hour with no luck.

"When we arrive, you will be sent to prison and then deported, unless you tell us where the money is."

Silence.

The criminal's bloodied body was carried out for all to observe. The crowd clapped and cheered.

Paolo and Placido brought in the second criminal. The captain and the first officer improved their act. After multiple beatings, the second delinquent finally admitted that he had not hid the treasure. The young man who had died took it because he had looked the most innocent. The second bruised and bloody body was thrown on the deck for all to see. Again, the crowd yelled with joy.

The third gangster knew his fate upon entering the captain's cabin. He admitted the same thing as the man before him: it was the young man who hid the treasure. To be consistent, they still threw out the third beaten body onto the deck. The crowd had not had this much entertainment throughout the entire journey. Their voices were louder each time a body flew out of the captain's door.

The fourth interrogation had really primed the captain and his first mate for questioning Max. This time, they went to their last, biggest culprit and took additional backup. All the men displayed their firepower or knives. The captain was warlike this round. He was determined to get the truth from this wicked man, after all the beatings with no results.

The captain took the most powerful gun and held it to Fortunati's head. The captain's eyes looked wide and crazy, his face flushed, and veins on his head and neck throbbed with fury. Paolo and Placido glanced at each other, shocked. The exchange was not lost on Max.

~ ~ ~

Finally they were getting somewhere. The priceless objects and money had been hidden in the bilges, where the storage lockers were. Antonino, Giovanna, Vincenzo, and Daniele rushed to them. They examined the rope lockers and the line lockers. No luck. The last lockers were the sail lockers. Under piles of material, they found oilcloth pouches. These sacks held the pirates' booty and the papal money. They jumped up and down and hugged. They materialized on deck with the oil sacks held high. Everyone rejoiced. The entire community would reap the benefits from these valuables.

As the crowd gathered that evening, Nino was lavish with compliments for the captain, the first mate, the crew, and all those who had helped to capture the members of the mafia clan. "Truly, we have many lionhearts among us, as my mother would say. I am honored to be on this journey with every one of you."

He requested that the captain and first mate demonstrate how they had handled the interrogations. The demonstration began with exaggerated, humorous antics. Of course, the best part was how they described dealing with Max.

Captain Scardino and his first mate chose Placido to portray Maximiliano. They were real comedians. Placido was being shaken and thrown around like a doll, which, of course, was a bit of exaggeration. Then, the captain added a gun and a huge saber to enhance the demonstration. Placido was screaming for mercy like a coward. The travelers shrieked with delight. Some bent over in laughter. It broke the tension of what was actually quite serious. They still had some days to go before they'd reach America and be able to turn them over to the authorities. They had to be kept secure.

CHAPTER 36

BRAVERY

The heroes approached Scardino and queried him about the treatment of the mafia men.

"Nino," he said, "do you know why you recognized Maximiliano from the university?"

"No," replied Nino. "Why?"

"Maximiliano was blackmailing a priest who taught there. The priest's family was wealthy, and his sister had been gravely indiscreet; every week Maximiliano collected blackmail money from the priest."

"The scoundrel!" Nino exclaimed.

The captain explained that when they landed in New Orleans, he would turn the gangsters over to the authorities. The officials would then deport them on the next ship returning to Sicily. "Good riddance to those evil men," the captain said angrily.

The group asked Scardino to announce to the other travelers what they should expect when they disembarked.

"I can tell you that we'll be stopping in Baldwin Port, in New Orleans very soon," the captain began. "It's much more humane for immigration checkups than Ellis Island in New York, but you'll have to wait in long lines and you'll receive little or no respect from the officers checking your papers and health. You'll be tired after the process.

"Afterward, find a couple with a sign that says, 'Newcomers' Help.' Papa and Mamma Tucci will provide you a comfortable environment and let you sleep at their center for as long as it is necessary. Mamma will have some hot food for you. You can pay them back by working for them. She and her husband are very good people. They work with the Catholic priest and their community."

"Thank you, captain, for all this information," Vincenzo responded. "Our next task will be to organize everyone who wishes to go with us, after lunch today."

Lunch came and went. The portions of food had become slimmer. Now was the time to get organized for the New World. Everyone came ready to work hard and fulfill their dreams of ample food on the table, some land of their own, and a little spending money.

One culturally embedded concept was that of continuous guilt about almost everything. Many of the travelers felt guilty for leaving their beautiful country. They did not want God to judge them as being ungrateful for their beautiful home. Some family members had told them they were defying God and committing a mortal sin by traveling to the New World.

The truth of the matter was that there were fewer jobs in Sicily, and the residents were experiencing starvation and hopelessness. More and more mobsters were asking for "protection money," because the economy was at an all-time low. That made it even more terrible for the people.

The men and women who left intended to help those at home as soon as they could by sending money. When they could afford it, they wanted to send for those who wished to come to America. In the meantime, they would faithfully devote their lives to the church and community in return for a good life in America. For them, it was the natural thing to do. The city would be designed with the church in the center of the development.

Antonino called for attention. Everyone became very quiet.

"Soon we will be landing in the Baldwin Port of New Orleans," he began. "It is located in the state of Louisiana. We will receive hot food, water, work, and lodging for three to four days at the Newcomers' Center. We will purchase seventeen wagons, seventy horses, livestock, and other supplies for the relocation of the fifty people coming with us.

"Our land is located by an established town called DeRidder. We will make that our temporary base while our town is being built. Anyone who has had experience with or studied how to plan or build a town, please come forward."

Three men stepped forward. They had hands-on experience with building houses and buildings in Sicily. One of them, Paolo, could survey the land and draw rough designs to work with the leadership team.

"Good," Antonino said, "Thank you. We'll meet with you after this meeting. Those who have been apprenticing with a team leader will continue to work with him or her for the next few days. If we need certain skilled people not in our group, we can recruit from the DeRidder townspeople.

"From what we can determine, we'll have approximately five square miles as our territory to develop. We'll build our town after considering many different opinions for its design. One town with one vision and strong mutual commitment to conserve God's natural gifts needs to be our philosophy. Ultimately, we'll have decent living conditions for those willing to work hard. Clean water and drainage will be important. It'll be a united approach, with the final decisions made by the leadership team.

"If you want to be a part of our community, please give your name to Placido, if you haven't already, and include what kind of skills you have. We'll meet again tomorrow morning. Spread the word to others, lest they be left out of the plan."

A large group of people stood in line to submit their name to Placido. There was a feeling of excitement and enthusiasm among the crowd. Their voyage was nearly over; their feet would soon touch land. The promise of a much better future was almost within their grasp. This is what they had asked for in their prayers. Many men and women came forward after the meeting, then milled around until Antonino called for them. Father Vincenzo began the dialogue by asking what their specific experiences had been. Interestingly enough, many had diverse skills and were anxious to go to work.

One of the men, Benito Deotto, had created gold-leafed ceilings, walls, saints, and figurines in his parish church. He had built an elaborate altar and pulpit for the priests. Besides having building skills, he knew how to work with metals, and he had designed chalices, holy medallions, lighting fixtures, doors, and a good many other things.

Another man, Dario Conti, asked to work on pews and kneelers because he had the expertise needed with wood. A third man, Remo Remotti, knew music and had built an organ for his home church. He had played for weddings, funerals, christenings, Masses, and the opera. Father Vincenzo was thrilled to have another musician.

Placido explained that he had experience with banking, accounting, and city planning. "I can also organize groups," he continued, "to accomplish many things." That talent had been demonstrated multiple times already.

Others came forward as firemen, barbers, masons, and many other diverse practical vocations. Nino and Vanna organized the new participants into already established groups for the afternoon activities. Vincenzo thanked the attendees for sharing their special gifts from God. The rest had two more days to get acquainted and decide if they wished to join the group. There was an overwhelming response to the invitation to travel to DeRidder. Placido and Vanna had all the names of the passengers who wanted to join them, organized in alphabetical order, including a list of their talents. Their last announcement was that the next morning, they would meet in groups. After that, they would clean the ship and get organized for their arrival. There was a happy buzz on the boat. Most could hardly wait to set foot in New Orleans. The next two days and nights went slowly.

What dreams would be materialized in the New World and what disappointments would become a reality? It would come down to *"Que sera, sera,"* ("Whatever will be, will be").

CHAPTER 37

IMMIGRATION

In the dawn, came that eventful day that the group had been waiting for with excitement, fear, collywobbles, dismay, and a re-examination of purpose: January 6, 1906. Fortunately, it was a Saturday, so the journey wouldn't be very difficult. Father led the congregation in prayer and distributed the sacrament of Holy Communion as the ship entered the New Orleans harbor. Conversations buzzed throughout the ship as they came closer to anchoring.

Plenty of noise arose from the shore. People cheered, called names, and shouted love messages. The train whistle and church bells could be heard among the rearing of horses and other livestock. It was a curious cacophony as the public health inspectors boarded the ship. With the help of the captain, they inspected passengers for diseases such as typhus, yellow fever, scarlet fever, bubonic or pneumonic plague, cholera, malaria, trachoma, or smallpox and hung a card on their coats if they passed. These particular diseases warranted a person to be quarantined. Thankfully, no one in their group had any of these afflictions.

Everything became a blur as the overdue passengers were herded into lines. Officials barked directions from bullhorns. For those who did not understand English, it was confusing and frightening. They simply followed the line and hoped they were doing the right things. They had to surrender their packs to strangers in uniform. They hoped the uniformed men could be trusted, unlike some of the men in the Sicilian regalia.

Hours passed, filled with humiliation. Each adult person had an Alien Registration Card hung around his or her neck while passing from line to line, which snaked off into the distance of an enormous warehouse-type building. Inspectors watched the gait and general appearance of every individual and started their exam at the feet. If there was a deformity or complication in a foreigner's limbs, he or she was ousted from the line, held, and deported.

A series of twenty or so questions were asked from the registry clerk with an interpreter, if an immigrant needed one. If an individual fell into certain categories such as dangerous or contagious, insanity or idiocy, he or she would be deported, as well as those who'd ever been to prison or housed in an institution.

The captain and crew informed the authorities about Max and his three malcontents and they hauled them to a holding cell.

Captain Scardino was on the other side of where the decision-making board was and he gathered together all those destined for DeRidder. Papa and Mamma Tucci were there, welcoming the group with open arms and kind voices.

The group walked two miles in freezing hail to get to the Newcomers' Center, which included a large hotel and dining hall to house and feed the new arrivals. Most were experiencing difficulty walking because of the needed adjustment from their "sea legs." When there, they had piping hot cocoa to drink with a delicious meal of polenta, cheese, and luscious tomatoes. It seemed they could not get their fill. Exhausted, everyone went to a bed much more comfortably in the hotel than in the wooden perches and floor of the ship. They drifted off to a sleep that felt like a coma. In the morning, they would have some orientation before getting to work.

CHAPTER 38

TRAVEL

Nino was the first to wake up, well before even the sun. He lay next to Giovanna thinking about how beautiful she was. It was impossible to remember her not being in his world. She was his wife, playmate, lover, best friend, and pillar of strength and security. Gazing at her made him feel as though his heart would explode with love.

Reflecting on all that they had been through thus far, Vanna had been by his side to support him in any way she could. He could not help smiling when he thought about how she had organized the women on the ship into the "Pots and Pans" troop when they had attacked Max and his men. That had taken creativity and courage. He stroked her silky brunette hair and kissed her gently on the cheek. She woke up with a beautiful smile, as was her nature.

The next several hours included anxious passion and then gentle, exhilarating lovemaking. They both knew what pleased the other, and they gladly expressed their intimate love. Soon, they hoped, Vanna would become pregnant.

Vanna said, "Nino, you are my pillar of love."

Breakfast was waiting for everyone as they slowly came into the dining area. There were ivory-colored tablecloths and fresh flowers on the tables. The smell of freshly brewed coffee permeated the room. Papa and Mamma Tucci had prepared fresh scrambled eggs with oregano, romano and parmesan cheeses, piles of buttered toast, crispy fried bacon, and garlic pan-fried potatoes. It was a delightfully charming American welcome.

Everyone was relieved and happy to be together again without the stress of the ship and its responsibilities. Even baby Sophia was extra joyful that morning. Gleefully, she drank the fresh milk and had bubbles and driblets running down her face. There was more food on her face than in her mouth. Everyone laughed at her with joy.

Within a half hour, Nino's group had been fed. Papa Tucci explained that the men would take on various responsibilities, such as plowing the fields, planting, and harvesting what was already matured. Some of the women and children could work in the refinery. Others could help clean the hotel rooms and the dining hall.

The cooking and baking group went to the market to buy ingredients within their budget for what they would be cooking during the next three days. These meals needed to be celebratory for their good fortune at arriving safely in America.

Upon their return, they made *brucciloni* (rolled stuffed steak with red gravy), chicken and rabbit cacciatore, fried calamari, lasagna, cannelloni stuffed with lamb, spaghetti and meatballs, and fried breaded chicken cutlets. Veal Parmesan with freshly made buffalo mozzarella cheese was a favorite. They stuffed sausages with ground beef, venison, wild pig, and lots of wine. Some sausages were put in a smokehouse. Seafood was very popular, including mussels, clams, oysters, and lobsters steamed in white wine, butter, parsley, and seasonings.

The bakers labored on some festive sweets. They made *sfingi* (donuts), *cassadini* (sweet ravioli), spumoni (ice cream with different flavors and colored layers, sometimes with fruit and/or nuts), marsala cake, tiramisu, and a plethora of yummy cookies. Some of the cookies were *cicilene* (sesame seed cookies), *cucidati* (fig-stuffed cookies), and *todos* (chocolate cookies).

Bread was another specialty. Some of the breads they concocted were plain and others had pepperoni or gorgonzola cheese. The dough was baked in clay ovens in which they used to cook all their food. It produced the most intoxicating scent. It wafted through the air, causing anyone in range to salivate.

Everything seemed perfect, until the wind started growing. The Tuccis excitedly told the Sicilians to retreat to the basement, because a tornado was coming. Many did not know what a tornado was. They explained the phenomenon, noting that one can cause devastation to entire cities.

"How long do they last?" asked Antonino.

"Anywhere from ten minutes to two hours," Papa Tucci said.

The group was in shock and many of the women cried. They had come this long way. *Would they be killed before their dream town was finished?* They waited in the basement nervously shaking until the Tuccis told them it was safe to come out. After a devastating hour, the barn was completely destroyed. After that, it became calm outside. The Tuccis assured them that it was safe to leave the basement.

They questioned if they had made the right decision of traveling to America. Mr. Tucci explained to them that they were fortunate this time for only losing a barn. In the past, they had endured much worse damage.

The cooks went back to producing their masterpieces; they drank wine, played music, sang, and teased one another. They then introduced the group to the townspeople who would be able to get them horses, covered wagons, blankets, cleaning items, cooking gear, food, wine, and other items they would need. After the tornado, the next three days were full of both merriment and hard work.

Later, Nino and Vanna spent some time writing to their families. They shared their experiences thus far and explained that they were leaving for DeRidder, Louisiana, very soon. They expressed how much they missed everyone and requested letters from home. Before they went to breakfast, they mailed their letters at the general post office. Afterward, the four leaders went to inquire about the land represented in the deed. They paid the fee to register the deed with the county and wondered how border disputes were resolved.

"We send out a surveyor," the clerk replied, "to clarify the boundaries."

How could it be that simple? Antonino wondered.

~ ~ ~

When January 10 came, everyone traveling to DeRidder was packed and ready to leave. The men were particularly careful that morning to put their right sock on first to ward off bad luck. They did not want to take any chances for the evil eye to interfere with their travel.

The Tuccis were sad that their guests had to go. They told the travelers that they were the nicest and liveliest group who had stayed with them. Nino assured them that they would keep in touch.

Traveling ten to fifteen miles was the goal of each day for the next few weeks, except for Sundays, of course, the day of rest. Any number of things, such as rain, mud, rivers, marshes, and bayous were unpredictable and could cause delays. Scouts on horseback would try to plan for what they could in advance of the wagon train and the travelers. They would travel along the Sabine River to Merryville, Louisiana, so they could have easy access to fish and water for the horses. The cooks would rise with the sun (or earlier) to make breakfast, and then everything would be loaded up for the day's journey. By late afternoon each day, they would have to stop to rest the horses so there was time to set up camp and cook dinner. And repeat.

As the seventeen wagons pulled out, many emotions went through the group: fear of the unknown, uncertainty of security, doubt about their future health, and homesickness, which would likely last for the rest of their lives. The one reassuring constant was that their four leaders would do the best they could to assist them all in realizing their dreams. They all had to have faith.

CHAPTER 39

GOOD FORTUNE

The group of fifty moved onward. It would be several weeks to get to Lake Charles, and another week to get to DeRidder. But building their own town was an exciting opportunity. That was their biggest incentive now.

The landscape was lush and green, and many of the plants were unfamiliar to the Sicilians. When the travelers stopped for an hour to rest, some people asked the leadership team to find out more about the flora, including the edible ones. The cooks were especially interested. Giovanna promised that she would find out more information along the way.

She had learned that there was a public library in Lake Charles. The North American Land and Timber Company had taken the initiative, through Austin V. Eastman, to build it. Andrew Carnegie had provided $10,000. There, she could learn about the flora and anything else interesting about Louisiana to teach her fellow travelers.

To ease the ordeal of the journey, adults tried to focus on looking forward to the "cutthroat card tournament" they had planned. The adults were already mercilessly teasing each other, threatening to bring their guns, butcher's knives, ropes, bows and arrows, or any other contraption they could think of to "scare" their opponents. Some pretended like they were going to cheat, and the others "threatened" their lives.

All the adults could play. The first night was designed to end up with sixteen finalists. Those finalists would then play the second night before the final winner was announced. The children thought they were so funny. Their parents and friends had not been so lively and silly in weeks.

Nunzio, Cuncetta, and the rest of the cooking group butchered a cow they'd purchased and delegated who would make what. Some were in charge of the spare ribs for barbecuing; the others made sausages, *bistecca pizzaiola* (steak, pizzamaker's style with pizza sauce), *bracciole* (stuffed beef rolls in tomato sauce), filet mignon, sirloin, ribeye steaks, standing rib roasts, and meatballs. They ate early so the silly yet ruthless card tournament could begin.

The leadership team organized eight groups. Everyone laughed so much that their stomachs ached and their eyes rolled out great quantities of tears. After Nino and Placido lost, they began the music. Those no longer in the game danced on the side. By midnight, there were only twenty players left. By one o'clock in the morning, sixteen finalists were named. The leaders had to figure out what the prize was going to be for the next evening.

The next day could not come soon enough for the finalists. A gold coin would be the prize. Chores were finished in record time. Giovanna told the students that they would end their lessons early that day.

Next, Nino signaled Vincenzo to clang the bell loudly to announce the finalists. The audience was very interactive; they hooted, hollered, heckled, clapped, and cheered for each person. The players took their "lucky" spots. One of the contestants proclaimed that he had worn his lucky underwear, so he could not lose.

The games began at six o'clock, and at ten, they were still playing. The group had been narrowed down to the final two players. Everyone was silent. In the next fifteen minutes, they would have a winner. The game was finally completed, and Benito, the gold leaf artist, was the champion. A goldsmith receiving a gold coin! He had been right; his lucky underwear had helped him win.

~ ~ ~

Every day during their rest periods, the leadership group held meetings to discuss the initial steps of planning their community. They had been told that Louisiana had a bureaucracy known as the Police Jury Commission, which made decisions for their territories. So, one of the first things they needed to do was meet with the police jury of DeRidder to explain their good fortune of securing a land deed and detail what their idea was for their land. If everything worked out the way they hoped, the police jury would approve their plans, then share the manpower they needed to build their territory. They wondered what the American government officials were like and how the process would work, as compared with what they knew.

Louisiana was divided into parishes, which had an administrative and legislative body that acted for the entire parish. Their members were elected from wards, or smaller divisions within the parish. There were no independent factions. The legislative powers regulated public works, internal police, safety, and livestock.

The Chief of Public Affairs operated out of a court-house. He had the responsibilities of the jail, hospitals, roads, drainage, ditches, levees, and sewerage. The chief's helper was the sheriff. Judges were considered ex-officio presidents when serving on the Police Jury Commission. Nino knew he had to tell everyone how the new area was operated and maintained, including who to ask if they had a question or if they needed to get permission to build something.

Daniele and Paolo would listen to the leadership team's ideas, along with the travelers and attempt to draft drawings that would reflect their thoughts of what their community should look like.

"Our beautiful church should be the center of the town," said Father Vincenzo. Industrialization, railways, roadways, water sewerage, the energy supply, and housing were topics of discussion. One of the issues they had to ponder was how they would be stewards of God's natural resources.

Their approach to the community had to be united. Many questions were posed throughout the discussions, including if there was sufficient area to build parks or gardens and if their buildings were appropriately symbolic of what their priorities as a community were. They also wanted to make sure that their land, while they hoped it could be seen as a work of art, was also true to their Italian heritage.

As they developed details of the town's design, they would hang the illustrations on the sides of the wagons at rest times for the rest of the community to see. Everyone was able to submit ideas. The first drawings were in ink on linen tracing cloth. Next, watercolor was added. Last, the drawings were stretched onto boards so they would be more permanent. Many of these would then be rendered and presented to the police jury. A proverb that seemed appropriate was "just when the caterpillar thought life to be over, it became a butterfly." They, too, were finding their wings.

As they traveled, they learned about their new country from people they met along their route next to the river. Lumbermen rafted logs on their way to the sawmill. Two men dressed in bib overalls operated a two-man saw. Men worked double-band saws, single cutting bands, edgers, and gang saws. The travelers also saw slip-tongued carts with mules pulling them.

Nino stopped to talk with the workers and learned that men made $3.50 a day as lumbermen or $7 a day as saw filers. The previous year there were three thousand box-cars full of timber transported to many destinations. This year, they were using Corliss steam engines to deliver their goods to sawmills. Sixteen miles of tram were built for the railroad, which extended well into the forest. The tram consisted of three pine-burning locomotives, with around fifty or sixty log cars.

The travelers' daily masses and novenas of prayers had helped them stay safe and travel at a decent pace, in spite of the rain and sleet. The wetness was frigid and it made one's bones ache and muscles shiver. Frost covered their wagons and their horses had to wear blankets to keep warm. When the blankets were soaked, others were put on the horses' back. A terrible case of the flu spread from one person to the next. Daniele and Rosina kept busy trying to keep everyone comfortable.

The days turned into weeks and the travelers soon found themselves at Lake Charles. Italians have traditionally been superior navigators and scouts; Placido and the others were no exception. Spirits were high and a party was planned for that evening, because the rain and hail had finally stopped. Everyone was wearing blankets, jackets, hats, and whatever else they had to keep them toasty. Fire pits were set up and the people rubbed their hands and stomped their feet to stay warm. Dancing was the thing to do; it helped warm the body. Hot, delicious food, and hot cocoa, coffee, and tea settled in their bellies nicely. They were almost able to forget about the cold.

While the group was enjoying their newfound freedom, during the next day of rest, Vanna invited Nino into the forest for a private picnic. She had thought of another way to stay warm. It had been too long since they had any private time, even though the Newcomers' Center helped to partially satiate their passion.

The wooded area was dense and their passion for one another was intense. Vanna promised not to let out a euphoric scream so that no one would come to their "aid." Her heart pounded and Nino began to sweat. The love they had for each other was addicting.

Nino whispered to Vanna, "I love you dearly. You are my pillar of refuge."

Afterward, they laid quietly beside each other. Neither one had anticipated how indescribably compatible they would be with one another. Nino stroked Vanna's gorgeous hair, while she gently moved her head to his chest. They napped for a short while, knowing that everyone would soon realize that two of their leaders had disappeared.

As they began to tidy up, Nino thought he saw something move in the undergrowth. He stood still, listening and staring for a while, but nothing moved. He reached for his hat on the ground. Then, seemingly out of nowhere, a Speckled King Snake lunged forward, headed right toward Vanna. She bit back a scream. Nino threw his hat at the snake. It emitted a foul-smelling musk. They had learned a bit about Louisiana snakes at the plantation. This particular snake was not venomous, but it had a reputation of being aggressive. Favored by rural folks because these snakes ate rodents and poisonous snakes, king snakes were referred to as the "salt-and-pepper" snake, because of the spots that covered their bodies.

Nino and Vanna ran quickly back to the camp. When they were almost there, they began to laugh deliriously. They agreed it would be a hilarious memory for years to come. Upon arrival, their friends asked if everything was okay, and they told them they had been running from a snake while they had been collecting kindling.

"You must have been really scared and dropped all your wood," someone said.

Vanna blushed.

They were camped next to a beautiful crystal-blue, cold lake. The children were the first to dive in. Their spirit was infectious. Some dove into the water, while others were pushed or thrown in. The group saw enormous trout.

Within seconds, Giuseppe and the fishing group geared up to catch the squiggly critters. They were so bountiful that one could almost catch them with bare hands. Within minutes, the cooks had their fry pans wetted with olive oil and wine with which to poach the trout.

After a refreshing swim for most, the dinner bell rang. With the myriad of tasty dishes, the travelers could only fit so much on their plates. It was necessary to go back to the buffet table several times. Then, of course, the dessert table needed a few turns, as well.

After everyone had their fill, Nino led everyone in a cheer for the hunters, fishermen, cooks, and bakers. The teenagers were fortunate that these talented people would spend their time teaching them gourmet techniques and seasonings.

Later, around the campfire, Vanna dramatically described her husband's valor with the snake. Nino swatted at the air and ran wildly around the fire, demonstrating his technique for the amused group.

Nino and Placido brought out their instruments to lull the children to sleep. Daniele played on his harmonica. Then, the dancing began and some started to softly sing. The wine was circulated, and everyone became sillier and sillier. They put all their effort into dancing the tarantella. It was quite a rendition, probably the first time they had ever danced it in the mud. Only people full of wine would dance that way. It was good therapy for them. They had not been able to indulge themselves like this for weeks. They stayed up much later than usual, dancing and laughing merrily into the night.

CHAPTER 40

RUSTLE

The sun was high in the sky the next morning by the time most were out of bed. Everyone bathed in the lake, even though the water was bone-chilling. The bakers started the bread in their portable clay ovens. The delicious smell floated on the light breeze into the forest and beyond. That was the hunters' cue to return to the camp. Soon, Daniele and the others brought back game birds and a large deer. Nunzio, Cuncetta, and the rest of their group butchered the game as best they could with their few knives.

The cooks were soon at it again. This time, they planned to barbeque the meat and concocted delectable marinades, seasonings, and flavorings to tenderize the meat. While the food was being prepared, many took a nap. Time seemed to be static as they drifted off to a snooze.

Giovanna had gone into town to use the library. At their meeting later that day, she was able to report what she had found out.

"Some of you have requested more information about the flora of Louisiana. Many of you are excellent farmers. Besides the cotton farming, some may want to farm sugarcane, potatoes, hay, fruits, vegetables, or blueberries, which are highly nutritious, and they could bring in a lot of money to our town. Other crops that are grown in abundance here are sweet potatoes, peaches, pears, tomatoes, bell peppers, squash, and cucumbers. Some flowers that love this environment are daylilies, roses, and gloriosa lilies.

"Knowing how expert many of you are as farmers, we are sure you will do well here. Since some of you are fishermen, there are fisheries in this area, and by working in one, you could bring in more money to our community. As we travel, you can reflect on what you would like to do to help our community, when it is built."

Two hours passed. Faintly, off in the distance, the horses stirred. Their snorting got louder. The sound of stampeding horses grew closer. Nino quickly realized what was happening. He grabbed the dinner bell and began clanging it as rapidly as he could to rouse the men.

"Horse rustlers!" Nino shouted. "Women and children to shelter! Men, grab any weapons you can find!

It seemed as though there were at least four horse rustlers. The horses that remained were quickly saddled so they could follow the thieves.

Large branches stuck out of the ground. Logs lay on their sides. Saplings and trees were dense. It was a challenging obstacle course. Sounds ahead alerted them that the thieves were not far away. When Paolo spotted the slowest rider, he lassoed him and forced him to the ground, searched him for weapons and removed them. Nunzio angled his whip to catch the next man's arm. The thug fell to the ground with a loud crash. Daniele captured the third criminal by grabbing the bridle of his horse. The horse reared and stopped.

Nino knew he needed to catch the fourth wretch. When he was even with the raider, it was difficult to seize him. They fell off their horses and struggled intensely in the dirt. It took three men to tie up the person. After they had securely bound him, everyone was amazed to find it was actually a woman they had captured.

The four renegades' hands and legs were tied, after which they were forced to walk back to Lake Charles. The men kept an attentive eye on the female, who was evidently the leader of the pack. No one spoke. These despicable people had not only stolen horses but food and supplies, as well. They were all tied to a wagon to ensure they would not escape.

After a fabulous dinner, the leadership team gathered to discuss what they should do with the thieves. They decided to bring the vagrants with them and turn them over to the sheriff in Merryville, a town on the way to DeRidder. In the meantime, the vagabonds would be restrained and guarded. Few had a restful sleep that night.

In spite of their frightful experience at the camp, the travelers advanced rapidly. They were determined to reach Merryville as soon as possible so that they could rid themselves of the horse thieves; but, it would still be several days. It was a stormy, blustery day. Only the scouts were out in this weather. Everyone else was riding in the wagons, which bounced mercilessly through the muddy, uneven terrain. Suddenly, a loud crack was heard. Someone's wagon had landed in a pothole and tipped over. A handful of men assembled around the wagon to determine what they should do. No one was hurt, but the accident had damaged the wagon.

Within minutes, the heroes were soaking wet. The family and their possessions would have to go in another wagon, as no one had the tools to fix the wagon. They had to leave the broken wagon there. The group again set out.

On the way to Merryville, the older children asked to ride in the same wagon together. They wanted to entertain the adults around the campfire with an opera. The adults shifted into the other wagons, as necessary. Some of the adults, including Vanna, Remo, and Vincenzo, helped plan the performance.

CHAPTER 41

DECEPTION

The wagons were posed in a circle later that afternoon so that everyone would be safe. Children played inside the circle. Guards were posted in strategic places. The adults went about their daily responsibilities washing clothes, sawing wood, grooming the horses, milking the goats and cows, decanting the wine for dinner, repairing the wagons, fetching eggs from the chickens, and running from the ferocious rooster who tried to peck at them; oftentimes he succeeded.

A gunshot punctuated the peaceful silence. A guard had fired on an escaped thief. Then, the female ruffian ran through the wagon circle wearing nothing but a smile. People were motionless and speechless, exactly what the thugs wanted. They commandeered a couple of the horses and picked her up. Once again, the travelers had been duped by these cunning criminals.

A cadre of men saddled their horses and went after the villains. It turned to late evening and there was no sign of them. Vincenzo led the community in Mass and prayer for the well-being of their leaders. Well into the night, the adults could not sleep.

Just as the sun was rising the next day, Nino and his followers arrived, quietly downtrodden. They had lost the trail of the horses. In spite of this loss, people at the camp all cheered them at their return. Their security was far more important.

"Let's be thankful they didn't steal any of the papal money," Vincenzo said. The men's wives clung to their returned husbands, with tears running down their faces.

Vanna said to Nino, "Don't ever leave me again. I will go with you, if it ever happens again. Nino, you are my pillar of security."

"You are the same for me, my love."

Exhaustion overtook those who had not slept the night before, so dinner was prepared later than usual, enabling them to rest. One more day of rest superseded keeping to the schedule. Before Vanna knew it, Antonino was snoring in their wagon.

A few days later, the wagon caravan, soaked through and through, stopped in Merryville. Men found a tarp for the cooks to have a dry spot to cook a full dinner and dessert. The travelers came out to get what food they wanted and then retreated into their wagons. No stars could be seen that night because of the thick rain clouds. Some played card games to pass away the evening; others sang or fell peacefully asleep.

The sunrise came much too early that day, but Merryville had the supplies that the travelers desperately needed. The leadership team helped people get settled. Everyone was feeling exhausted and inquisitive about their destination.

The leaders of the town were friendly and were more than willing to speak with these new immigrants. They exchanged stories of the wilderness and the surrounding area. Nino asked the townspeople if they knew anything about a group of criminals. He explained how four bandits had stolen a few of their horses, and some of their supplies. He described them in great detail, emphasizing the wild female leader.

One of the residents shared that he had seen a group of low lives that fit Nino's description. They had been going in a northeastern direction two days before. From Merryville, that was in the direction of DeRidder. The leadership team hoped they would catch up to them there. When the group returned to the wagons, Nino sent out ten scouts, including Placido, Paolo, Benito, and Dario, to go ahead of the wagon train, with the mission of capturing the criminals. About ten miles out, Benito saw tracks that could have been the robbers'. They sped in that direction. Later that evening, they slowed down because they had discovered a campfire. They dismounted and crept quietly toward the light. Placido directed them to surround the area, and, on a birdlike signal, they were to throw blankets over the heads of the scoundrels.

The defendants screamed and fought back.

"Merda, porco cane!" ("Shit, for God's sake!")

They lifted the blankets in surprise of hearing Italian. These people were only a family, a father and his three sons out hunting. The campfire light had played tricks on their eyes, allowing them to see only what they had wanted.

The captors apologized and explained who they were tracking. The father willingly shared that his family had seen the drunken mob a few hours before they had set up camp. Probably because their family was poor, the robbers had not been interested in stealing from the man and his sons. One of the older sons said he thought the vagrants were headed for DeRidder. The thoughtful Italians offered some of their delicious food to them, hoping to make amends. Not only did the family accept the offerings, but they also volunteered to help with the reconnaissance.

When the sun was rising the next morning, they headed out, hell-bent on capturing the burglars. It was a cold, dry day. Benito led the group as they scoured the countryside. A small lake was nearby. *Voices!* Sure enough, they saw the backs of the shameful lot through the bushes. Placido motioned his followers to grab the clubs they had made. In unison, they got in groups of three and four and attacked the thieves. There was much scurrying around and fists flew. With three against one, however, the struggle ended quickly. Still, it took more manpower than expected to take down the female.

The four were bound and made to walk back to Merryville. It took most of the day, but it was not difficult, thanks to Benito's keen sense of direction. The sheriff instructed them to bring the prisoners to DeRidder, because it had a jail. The group returned to their friends. The dad of the three boys, Fabio, asked if they might join their group. He explained that his wife and daughter had died in childbirth some weeks prior, and they were now aimless. The leadership team welcomed assistance from their fellow Italian countrymen.

The prisoners were tied at the hands and feet and pushed into a wagon with multiple guards. There was no way that they could escape this time. Everyone slept, except the guards, who knew this time to take turns.

CHAPTER 42

PERFORMANCE

Most everyone the next morning was refreshed and rested because of their quiet night. The travel schedule provided for another day of rest and relaxation. Most bathed in a marshy lake, or bayou, knowing they still had quite a journey ahead of them that day, or maybe two, before they reached DeRidder. The fishermen were out securing dinner from the slow stream. While fishing, they observed lumbermen cutting down trees in the compact, overgrown pine forest that had cypress trees interspersed.

Soon the travelers were packing up their belongings. The adolescents were ready to perform their comical opera that night, *The Barber of Seville*. Vanna, Vincenzo, Dario, and Nino had a deep appreciation for music and they wanted their community of friends to enjoy it with them.

Permission from Nino for the youngsters to perform that evening came as a delight. Some of the youngsters introduced the opera and the performers. Giovanna, Remo, and Father Vincenzo were given credit as the directors.

The performers' arias and voices were beautiful. The applause was roudy. Impatiently, they waited for the second act. During their break, everyone enjoyed gazing at the stars. It had been some time since the night sky had been clear enough to appreciate the twinkling lights. The masterful job made the adults realize what gifted children they had. They had organized themselves, and, with help, had learned the plot and the music.

Vanna had made learning fun, and in the process, from the boat to now, everyone in the group had learned to read at some level. Adults and children had faithfully come to her classes. Through literacy, they could also truly love and appreciate all that Italian culture had to offer them: roots, love, family, an indomitable spirit, fun, books, playing instruments, dancing, cooking, and the Italian zest for life. That night, everyone went to bed with light hearts.

The next morning, the travel they had to accomplish that day now seemed easy. At every possible opportunity, the adults praised the performers for their outstanding opera. More people were singing that day than usual.

CHAPTER 43

OPPORTUNITIES

The travelers were disciplined in their schedule. They were nearing DeRidder and their excitement was growing with every mile traveled. Before they began the last leg of their journey, Nunzio and Placido gathered everyone for a meeting. Vincenzo opened the meeting with Mass. After they had all received Holy Communion, the conference began.

Antonino started with comments on all the accomplishments the group had performed, even under duress. Giovanna disclosed information she had found while researching America in general, and DeRidder, so that everyone would be familiar with their new surroundings.

The president of the United States was Theodore Roosevelt. The town had been named after Ella DeRidder, who was the sister-in-law of a Dutch railroad financier. In 1893, there had been a very serious financial panic. Many railroads went bankrupt. DeRidder's railroad, however, had pulled the economy out of its hole, and it continued to expand its reach. It had drawn many people to the area, and various industries, such as lumber, had expanded.

Daniele continued, explaining background information about DeRidder's history. "When the Confederates lost in the Civil War, many Louisiana veterans invested in the turpentine industry. Turpentine was volatile and had many uses, including as a paint thinner and solvent. Its biggest derivative, pine oil, was used as a disinfectant. The turpentine business needed barrels. Barrel-making became a lucrative business itself. These may be jobs to consider."

"The first Telegraph Office was the Western Union, opened in 1870; the first home had been built in 1893, and it had been made out of logs and board shingles. They had been split by hand from the largest pine trees in the world. In 1898, the first post office was built. The first school was built in 1899. The first train to DeRidder was the Pittsburg and Gulf Railroad, which had arrived in 1902." Then, Daniele beckoned Vincenzo to say a few words.

Antonino concluded the meeting by giving the signal for everyone to get into their wagons. Moments later, the exhausted, yet persistent people began the last part of their journey. The group began singing favorite Italian songs to pass the time, filling their hearts with joy.

CHAPTER 44

REMEMBRANCES

The captives, under heavy guard, were yelling, attempting to drown out the beautiful songs. When their voices grew hoarse, they finally stopped. They begged for water, but the guards refused. In retaliation, the criminals began jumping up and down in the wagon to throw the horses off balance. This lasted for about two miles, after which, they began pounding their heads against the wagon's walls. The guards were dismissive.

That day they would stop for lunch instead of dinner, in the hopes of reaching DeRidder that night. At break time, the wagons formed a circle. The barbequed venison had a tantalizing aroma. The female bandit began howling like a wild coyote. Giovanna had a soft heart and asked the leadership team to at least give them water. They reluctantly did.

After lunch, the community started down the Confederate roads again. Birds chirped among the sound of raindrops. Some of the birds seemed to be dancing together in the wind. The young ones chased each other in circles among the clouds.

"I was thinking if it would be okay to call you 'Tony,' too," Vanna said. "It sounds more American." He responded favorably and asked her if he could call her "Gio," pronounced "Jo." It, too, sounded more American.

Tony and Gio were more nostalgic today than usual. Maybe it was the weather. They snuggled on the wagon bench, professing their deep love for each other. Tony leaned down and kissed Giovanna tenderly on the forehead. The travelers on horses enjoyed seeing the happy couple. Tony repeated his wedding vows to Gio as he did every day. He asked her if she was thinking of her family in Sicily. She could not deny it. So was he.

"I wonder what they're thinking and doing now," he said. "Mamma and my sister are probably baking fresh bread for dinner and making a salad with tomatoes, mozzarella, basil, thyme, and oregano. Papa would be hunting for rabbits. Our dog, "Polpette" ("Meatball"), would probably be digging up truffles for the macaroni and cheese. What do you think your family is doing right now?"

"I believe my father and brothers would be deciding which wine to serve for dinner," Gio replied. "Mamma and my sisters would be cooking a huge amount of food to donate to the church. Later today, they'd join others to feed the hungry parishioners. Then they'd go back home and eat. Since it's a Sunday, Cardinal Cusimano, Bishop Lucchessi, and Father Primo would be invited. I know they'd be expressing thanks for the incredible food and praying for us. Then, Papa would play his harmonica and my brothers would accompany him with their accordion or squeezebox, drum, and violin. Mamma would lead the singing." Tears rolled down Gio's cheeks. *Will missing home ever not hurt so much?*

CHAPTER 45

ARRIVAL

The morning had been filled with high hopes that they would arrive in DeRidder that evening. In fact, it was close to midnight when they finally arrived. Even though it had been very difficult traveling in the darkness, the scouts had held lanterns and led the group on the path ahead. They were determined not to stop until they had reached their new home. When they arrived, lighting from the streetlamps made the roads beautiful, twinkling like a fairy-land. Slowly, they formed a wagon circle. Most went to bed without dinner, because their fatigue was so severe.

The first order of business that coming morning would be to turn over the captives. The leadership team and Placido located the government building, found the police jury commissioners, and explained who they were and why they had come. The members of the police jury introduced themselves and welcomed the new residents. The middle-aged Robert Smith was in charge. Gio related the criminals' misdeeds and Tony then asked the jury members to escort the four villains to prison.

Robert responded, "Certainly. We have what we call 'the hanging jail.' Many criminals have been convicted and hanged here."

"Be sure to bring your guns," she warned. "They're very wild and the female is nearly impossible to control."

"We'll walk back to the wagons with you, so you can take charge of the four rogues," Tony said. "Our cooks will make lunch for you while you're there. You're always welcome to eat with us."

On the way back to the wagons, the leadership team alternated telling the townspeople their mission, the vision for their plot of land, their travel experiences, and the expertise of their community.

A downpour started just as they arrived at the wagons. Quickly, the travelers organized themselves. A tarp was hung for the cooks and the bakers. The musicians started playing favorite songs while they served their best red wine. Everyone was having a great time, except for the guards and the captives.

The scoundrels' feet had been bound together, but they began kicking the insides of the wagon. Boards came loose; Placido and the town's authorities arrived just in time to relieve the guards. They put their guns in the mouths of the criminals, showing that they would not tolerate misbehavior. Immediately, the kicking ceased.

The lunch was fantastic. Everyone, including the guards, enjoyed the food immensely. The police had never had raviolis and meat sauce. They could not get enough of the delicate little pillows. The leadership team gave up their raviolis to the police, to try and satisfy them. Dessert was an Italian cake, which consisted of a white cake, butter, buttermilk, egg whites, and pecans. Whenever a cake was served, Tony always said, "I'm not talking while the flavor lasts." It took three pieces of cake to get the leadership team to speak again.

A tour was planned for the immigrants at noon the following day. The owner of the lumber company came out to welcome the town's guests. He bragged that he paid in legal currency, rather than in tokens or mill checks, in an attempt to recruit workers. Workers received cash and did not have an extra step to get their money by going to the bank.

He told them that last year, 1905, he had shipped a half million feet of pine and cypress boards. That almost seemed impossible, but when the journeyers looked around at all the trees, they knew it was not that hard to believe. The group also saw a few automobiles, which shocked most of them.

They also saw a waterworks and were impressed that some parts of the town had electricity. Louisiana had many ice manufacturing businesses. The cooks, farmers, bakers, hunters, ranchers, the clinic personnel, and the grocery store would need ice for refrigeration, and an ice plant was considered a utility long before electric lights, natural gas, or running water. Small steam engines were used to generate electricity to run the ice companies' motors. Ice companies also used the power to light their plants. They sold excess energy to nearby homes and businesses in the evenings. Their town would be one of the lucky recipients of electricity, natural gas, and running water.

And phones! By 1900, there were 600,000 phones in the United States. By the time 1905 came, there were 2.2 million phones in the United States, and the immigrants' community would be included.

DeRidder was only nine years old and it had been incorporated into Louisiana in 1903. Methodist and Baptist churches had been established there. The Sicilian group saw muddy roads, artesian wells, a bank, an iron foundry, an inn, and an opera house, which pleased them enormously. Because their land deed was bordered by DeRidder, they could access all of these resources.

Tony showed the purchased land deed to Robert, explaining that they wanted to build a community on their land and that they were requesting the city's help. Robert instantly liked the Italian citizens. He readily agreed to help them.

Tony thanked them for their assistance and they scheduled another meeting in a week.

Robert planned to come often for lunch, dinner, or both. Gio asked if he was interested in meeting a woman to marry who cooked. "That's a nice idea!" Robert responded.

Gio invited Giullietta over to meet Robert. She was embarrassed, but she truly wanted a husband. Giullietta had traveled alone on the ship. She was young, quiet, and shy. As soon as the work groups had been formed on the ship, she had joined the cooking group.

Robert saw the two women coming toward him. Next to Gio was a petite young woman with an olive complexion and deeply set black eyes. Her hair was pulled back in a bun and her eyes twinkled with happiness. Her smile was irresistible.

After meeting her, Robert asked Tony if he could return the following night for dinner to get to know Giullietta. Tony and Gio smiled. Robert knew at that moment that he wanted Giullietta as his wife.

CHAPTER 46

GETTING ACQUAINTED

Giullietta was nervous the next day. She felt responsibility to keep this important official in their good graces for the benefit of their community. She had decided to make her specialty dinner for Robert. First, she made large, round, flat cannelloni crepe pasta. She cooked her tomato sauce all day with hunks of venison and pork. Then she stuffed the pasta with the tomato sauce, cheese, and meat, rolling it over in the pan to secure the stuffing. Handmade garlic bread would accompany the pasta. For the grand finale, her group made tiramisu.

She bathed, shampooed her luxurious hair, and put on her only nice dress in anticipation of her suitor's presence that evening. Unfortunately, because he was the town's head jury policeman, he had been called away to deal with some criminals in the area. Giullietta was disappointed, but at least Rosina and baby Sophia always cheered her up.

Nino asked her if she would be happy with a husband who was called away so frequently. Being young and naive, she replied unconvincingly that she would be.

"He's such an honorable and respected man," she said. "It would be a privilege to be his wife." Giullietta changed her clothes and disappointedly ate dinner with the rest of the community. The supper was so good that Tony suggested a plate of it be delivered to Robert so that he could enjoy it, too. Fabio Testi, the man who had been found with his sons in the wild, offered to deliver it.

Fabio rode an outstanding Arabian horse named *Campione* (Champion), who was black as midnight except for the white star on his forehead. His mane was braided meticulously and the last foot of it fell loosely on his back. When he ran, his tail and mane floated in the wind. The immigrants had never seen a horse comparable to *Campione*. Fabio returned after some time and announced to Giullietta that Robert had been delighted with her cooking. He had asked Fabio to tell her that he would come for dinner the next night to see her.

Giullietta began planning the next evening's meal with the cooks. She asked Tony if it was okay to prepare veal saltimbocca. It was an extravagant meal, but he wanted Giullietta to impress Robert, so he said she could. She hurriedly told the others and began marinating the meat so that it would be ready the next evening. The course required that the meat be extra tender because it needed to be stuffed, rolled, and sautéed in white wine, capers, and roasted red bell pepper sauce. Word spread quickly what was being prepared for the next day.

Fabio had joined the cooks' team to help Giullietta. He lifted heavy pots for her and prepared the dressing for the pilaf. The dressing had olive oil, flavored vinegars, honey, garlic, and orange juice. It was a combination of orzo and rice. The starches had to be boiled in chicken broth with onion, celery, and parsley. When completely cooked and drained, dried fruit and toasted pecans were added. Fabio mixed the ingredients together with the dressing in a huge pot.

Giullietta watched Fabio work. She couldn't resist asking him who had taught him to cook. He responded that his wife had taught him. His plan was working. He had wanted her to notice.

"My wife died, and I have had to provide for my three sons, Edoardo, Pietro, and Stefano, ever since. Cooking has been one of my responsibilities," he replied. Giullietta wanted to know more, but she felt it would be too forward to ask more questions.

She followed yesterday's routine. She bathed, shampooed her hair, and let it fall in ringlets around her face. She put on her only nice dress. She took some of the dried fruit, soaked it in water, and rubbed it on her cheeks and lips. The extra color was very becoming to her features. She was nervous and excited that Robert would attend the meal.

He was greeted with flags and musical pageantry by the new residents. They were honored to have the city's highest ranking official in their midst. He greatly enjoyed the gourmet meal, as did everyone else. Tony, Gio, Vincenzo, Daniele, Rosina, Giullietta, Fabio, Edoardo, Pietro, Stefano, and Robert all sat at the same table. Robert inquired who had put the meal together. Naturally, Tony started with Giullietta's name, when mentioning those on the cook's team. Because Fabio had just joined the group with his sons, Giullietta felt it necessary to discuss the help he had afforded her. Robert complimented the cooks.

The cleanup crew began clearing plates. That was an opportunity for Robert to ask if Giullietta would like to walk with him a bit.

"Since her parents aren't here, we will go along as her chaperone," Gio said, assuming that Robert didn't know their courting customs.

The strong scent of pine trees along the walk was pleasant. The whispering of the river was melodic and refreshing. Gio had always enjoyed the sound of frogs; she recalled for the group when Tony had hidden a frog in her lunch basket at school. Everyone laughed.

Tony discussed Giullietta's fine qualities, which seemed to impress the officer. They asked questions of Robert, too, so that everyone could become better acquainted. Then, Gio bragged about Giullietta's gourmet cooking. Her aunt had taught her a lot, because her mom had been an invalid. Robert inquired about her mom.

"I hope you don't feel I am being too aggressive in asking," he said.

"Not at all," Giullietta responded. "My mother was the best mother anyone could ever be blessed enough to have. Her passion in life was helping others. One day, she witnessed a mafia member beating a young orphan boy. She rushed to defend him. The gangster, instead, whipped my mother. He left them bleeding out in the street.

"Bystanders found them and ran to get my brothers, who carried the two bodies home. My father was hysterical and called a doctor. His initial reaction was to get revenge. She begged him to forgive the demented man. My father didn't want to comply, but he loved my mother too much to go against her wishes. We had ten children in the family, and my parents made it eleven by adopting the maimed boy. My mother and the boy never walked again."

She continued. "Even through all her pain, my mother smiled and sang because by doing so, she believed she did the work of Jesus. She performed her duties that didn't require walking. She was the perfect role model for everyone. I'm grateful that my mother taught me so many lessons."

"Yes, indeed," Robert said. "You're very articulate and mature for your age." She smiled and blushed. The foursome soon arrived back at the campsite. Meanwhile, the group had planned entertainment for Robert.

Tony started playing his mandolin, Placido began on his squeeze-box, and the others accompanied them with the harmonica and the drums. The group began singing traditional Italian songs. Robert asked Giullietta to dance. She was embarrassed, but she accepted his offer. He was muscular, tall, slender, confident, and a skilled dancer. He was not easily impressed, but it was obvious that he admired Giullietta. Her curly hair tossed about as they danced.

Giuseppe, Angelina, and baby Sophia danced with the crowd. People could hear Sophia's happy baby squeals. Daniele and Rosina loved to dance, in spite of his disability.

After the dancing, Fabio and his sons put on a horse show. *Campione* jumped through hoops of fire, reared on his back legs as high as the sky, jumped hurdles with ease, and counted to five by stomping his hoof on the ground five times. The champion horse reminded Tony of his mother's beautiful horse, Precious.

"What a magnificent animal," Tony said.

Fabio is pretty magnificent himself, Giullietta thought. *Hush, sweet thoughts.*

The audience was spellbound by *Campione's* dressage, what Fabio termed "horse ballet," and they cheered loudly for his performance.

Fabio informed the group that he had purchased *Campione* in New Orleans in an area where the Creoles lived. Someone in the crowd asked, "What is a 'Creole'?"

"The Creoles live in Southern Louisiana, around New Orleans," explained Fabio. "You probably saw them when you were there, but you just didn't know who they were. Criollo is a Spanish term that means 'local.' These people are a mix of the slaves brought to the United States from West Africa and Europeans who married African, Haitian, and people from the West Indies. Their intermarriages created the Creole culture.

"Now, for his last demonstration for the evening, *Campione* will race to the end of the camp and return with lightning speed." The spectators gave the horse and Fabio a standing ovation. The crowd knew they had to rise early to work, so they all scurried off to bed when the show concluded.

CHAPTER 47

DETERMINATION

The next day, the foursome planned their meeting agenda for the Police Jury Commission. Giullietta had baked hot biscuits for the meeting; butter and fig preserves were added, with a container of clabber for Robert's breakfast. For lunch, Giullietta had plucked a chicken and fried the pieces, adding dumplings on the side. There was enough for all of them to devour.

Gio began by clarifying the process they had employed, allowing all fifty-plus citizens to have an opportunity to share their ideas.

Father Vincenzo explained the general layout for the new territory. The team wanted the center of it to be similar to how Washington, DC, was planned, with a beautiful, domed rotunda, which would be on their basilica, at the center.

"Leading up to the basilica, we would like to plant oak trees lining both sides of the road. The trees would be trained to bend on top, forming an archway to the basilica, allowing everyone in the future to marvel at the spectacle done for God." They had noticed a plantation on the way from New Orleans called "Oak Alley," and they wanted it to be similar. This would be built with a rectory. The axial roads would be arranged in a star shape.

Daniele and Rosina showed one of the large drawings. It rendered the skeleton of the town's center, complete with all the sewage pipes and electrical lines. Electrical lines would be tied into the large ice company. In return, the Sicilians would help the company install the necessary lines. The commission members were impressed with all the planning the group had done.

Nino was next. His task was to describe the businesses they would be able to open based on their group members' experience. Trees would need clearing for their farmland, and that would require the help of the DeRidder lumber company.

Ordering and inventorying all their supplies would be assigned to Gio and Vincenzo, including all the supplies needed for the church. They would need experts to help them with ordering supplies, which needed to be done immediately, so that when better weather came, they would be able to begin building. They wanted the entire project to be completed in six months.

The next display was reviewed by Daniele. It contained the job skills for each type of work, and every journeyer's name was listed next to his or her occupation. The commission also volunteered skilled laborers looking for work, if needed.

Tony explained that in Sicily, the family was a strong defense in the desperate effort to survive. In America, there would be no competition between families. Everyone would support each other rather than compete with each other. Resolutely patriarchal, the Sicilian family deferred to the father on every decision. The mother's role was also important; while she did not possess an equal share of authority, she, nevertheless, had the important task of running the household. They had a fixed set of cultural rules. For example, the first male child born was named for the father's father, and the first girl was named after the father's mother. Sons and daughters afterward were named for the mother's father and mother.

Tony explained that men's, women's, and children's roles would have to be adjusted here. Women would continue to be able to participate in decision making, as they began on the ship. Children would also help the adults when they turned twelve. They would go to school until that age, or longer, if the parents agreed. To build their community, everyone needed to work.

Daniele showed the last painting. It was a depiction of what the town would look like when finished. Their audience had enough foresight to know that this new town was going to help the entire area.

"There are only two other topics we need to discuss," Tony explained. "If you have other subjects to discuss, please let us know. The next issue necessitates a discussion of budget and money. Long-term, we may need some assistance monetarily; however, we have enough to get our city started. We need to know prices for equipment, supplies, and salaries. After we get this information, we'll present a formal budget to you. We assure you that we'll be judicious in our decision-making procedures.

"The last item on our agenda is the name of our new town. We're all homesick for our treasured Sicily, so we'd like you to support the name of 'Little Sicily.' What do you think?"

There was a hush in the room. The commission members looked to Robert for a response.

"We can support that name with trepidation," he responded slowly. "Unfortunately, there are some community members who are prejudiced and hostile toward other immigrants. Give it time. Establish businesses. If you can become part of the economy, money can open doors in America."

With that being said, Tony asked if another meeting could be scheduled to discuss the budget and the existing prejudices. The commission avowed that the next meeting would be scheduled for one month from the current date, with any other agenda items to be added the week before the gathering. The leadership crew politely thanked the group for their attentiveness and participation. Robert found a convenient moment to ask if he might join them for dinner that night. The response was that the commission members were always welcome.

CHAPTER 48

COMMUNICATION

Giullietta anticipated that Robert would come for dinner. As a result, she had proposed to the team that they make pasta and peas to balance the excessiveness from the night before. The dessert would be apple bread pudding. Fabio and his sons inquired if they could help. Giullietta was impressed by the boys' politeness.

He has raised those boys to be gentlemen, she thought. They set the tables with cloths, utensils, and flowers. She set her place in the middle, as unmarried women were not to sit at the end of a table, or they would never marry. Daylight was now lasting longer. The climate was similar to their cherished Sicily.

When Robert arrived, he had a gift for Giullietta. It was a new, expensive frying pan. She was appreciative of his thoughtfulness. He seemed more handsome than usual that night. There was a certain glow in his eyes and a sparkle in his smile. Each visit seemed more comfortable than the last.

Before everyone knew it, a month had passed, and it was time for the next meeting with the officers. Gio and Vincenzo had worked night and day with distributors to figure out the pricing and quantities of their needed supplies. They found it easy to work together, because they were both organized and focused on details.

As a trained surveyor, Paolo would decide which roads went where, and the Sicilian group had begun digging utility trenches immediately after the last meeting; consequently, an agenda item was to have their work inspected and approved by the commission. Gio and Vincenzo presented an itemized budget that demonstrated their effort to be as exact as they could at this stage in the project.

Questions ensued. Gio and the priest answered them confidently. The officers suggested fundraising to cover the shortfall. That topic would be explored more in the next meeting. Uncomfortable as it was, Tony brought up the issue of prejudice. From all that they had read, the United States of America was a land where diversity abounded. He asked if they misunderstood the intent of the Declaration of Independence.

The second in command, John Crockett, had been born in Louisiana, and responded. "Differences sometimes lead to suspicion and mistrust when there is a lack of understanding. In our area, there has been little exposure to your way of life; therefore, it will take time for people to adjust."

John then told a story about integrated workers being side by side in the trenches, sharing food, drinks, and casual conversation. It had already changed some of the DeRidder workers' attitudes about the "WOPs" ("WithOut Passports"); that term was disdainful, and most of the Sicilian group did not know what it meant.

Other slang for Italians included "grease balls," "dagos," "giappo" (pronounced "joppo," meaning "thug"), and "guineas." Actually, the term "dago" was not originally derogatory. The term had referred to those who spoke Italian, Portuguese, or Spanish.

"The ideal of every person's potential being realized is a hard concept to implement," John said, "but it'll come more easily with time. The people in the DeRidder community will begin to realize that what they hold dear is the same for the immigrants: family, acceptance, belonging, and love." Applause erupted.

"We have a determination to succeed," Tony continued. "Perhaps after today's presentation, you all might help us in spreading successful stories of Italians in history. You've mentioned that many of the folks here aren't educated. This is an opportunity to educate them. You could discuss the Roman Empire, Galileo, Marco Polo, Leonardo Da Vinci, Michelangelo, Christopher Columbus, Amerigo Vespucci, Filippo Mazzei, or many others. The notion of 'all men are created equal' originated from Mazzei. If you need to review these peoples' successes, we would be happy to conduct a class."

The commission members liked this idea. In exchange, the team requested that the ideals of American culture be shared. For the last agenda item, the immigrants needed information about Baptist and Methodist beliefs.

The Baptist and Methodist commissioners explained that the religions shared doctrines with Catholicism. Vincenzo articulated an extraordinary discovery: Christianity is a universal church and all Christians need to spread the love of God. The meeting concluded with applause for Father Vincenzo.

To further their goodwill, the leadership troop invited all the council members and their spouses to dinner the following night.

The class would be scheduled for the following Tuesday morning at nine o'clock in the city's chambers. Fundraising would be postponed as a topic until the next meeting, in two weeks. The foursome felt that they had made significant progress with the DeRidder leaders.

Two weeks went by; meanwhile, the work went on in three eight-hour shifts. Electricity from the ice plant allowed the immigrants to work the evening and midnight shifts with ease. Progress seemed slow at first, but soon, all of the necessary underground work had been completed. Their new territory was going to have all the modern comforts. The DeRidder people were impressed by the quality of their companions' work and their knowhow.

The third meeting with the officers began with an expression of gratitude that they had inspected and approved the completed work. Secretly, they were amazed that they hadn't needed to monetarily "convince" them that the work was up to standards. Gio and Vincenzo provided a status report of the budget and the necessary changes that needed to be implemented. It was an abbreviated report, because only a few items had been altered.

Daniele and Rosina addressed the group. Daniele explained that he was a doctor and that Rosina was a nurse. Part of their plan was to build a clinic and expand it into a hospital when it became possible. Daniele requested the group to think about any other needs the city had and asked the commissioners to spread the word about the new jobs that would develop as a result of their clinic and other aspects of their city.

"Some of the new jobs will probably include: black-smiths, photographers, lumberjacks, firemen, milliners, launderers, barbers, and hotel manager, among others," he said.

Daniele inquired what skills and talents the DeRidder occupants had. The list was long. There was no intention of replacing the immigrants with the Americans in their jobs; however, there would be a genuine consideration of hiring Americans when necessary.

Vincenzo concluded the meeting, asking everyone to bring fundraising ideas to the leadership group. The tradition of inviting the jury commissioners to dinner had already been established, so of course, they were again invited. They were excited, because they had long since realized how much they enjoyed the immigrants' cooking. Robert was especially happy to go.

After the meeting, he questioned Tony and Gio about when would be an appropriate time to ask for Giullietta's hand in marriage. They suggested that they speak to Giullietta first, and then they would get back to him with an answer. Robert could hardly wait for dinner.

CHAPTER 49

TORMENT

Giullietta had never tasted such delicious rabbit as in the special sauce Fabio had cooked it in.

"If the hunting team helps you and your sons trap enough rabbits," she asked, "will you teach me how to make this sauce for tonight's supper?"

I would enjoy that very much," he said.

Within three hours, the hunters returned with an abundance of rabbits. The next step was to take the cooking team into the forest and show them which herbs to pick for the sauce. After Giullietta finished churning the butter, Fabio demonstrated how to mix the sauce. It was a Cajun seasoning combination of paprika, wine, onion, salt, garlic, pepper, bell peppers, chilies, mustard, cumin, thyme, oregano, sage, celery, butter, and wine. The meat cooked for several hours in the wine sauce. They would serve the rabbit with rice and beans. When vegetables were added, the end result was a delicious jambalaya stew.

The immigrants had never heard the terms Cajun and jambalaya. Fabio told them the story of the Cajun culture as it had been explained to him.

"Fifteen years before the Mayflower landed," he began, "people migrated from Nova Scotia into northern Louisiana. These folks were fun-loving and hard-working. They had a zest for life and it describes their culture perfectly. They typically play lively music with accordions, fiddles, and triangles. At their festivals, they have music with dancing and a parade of masked and costumed horses and riders. A featured food is always jambalaya."

Most of these Cajun people had been uneducated. The immigrants felt sorry for them because they had been ridiculed and called disrespectful words. "Some had called them a 'swampbilly' because they lived in shanty house-boats," he said.

After his explanation, Giullietta showed her upper arm to Fabio, tensing her muscles to enlarge them.

"That's what happens with all the pumping of the churn to make the butter," she said. They both laughed.

It was time for her to freshen up before Robert arrived. When she was just about ready, Gio knocked on her wagon. She asked for her to come and discuss an important matter. She thought she might have some idea of the subject.

Tony began, "Robert has asked for your hand in marriage."

"Oh," was her only reply.

"Are you willing to marry him? If so, when?" Gio asked.

"I . . . don't know. I need to think about it," Giullietta responded hastily. Tony and Gio were astonished. They did not want to force her answer, but they wanted to know when she would decide. They reminded her how important it was to their community to have local officials on their side.

"Please give me forty-eight hours to think about it," she said.

Later that night, Tony shared her answer during a private moment with Robert. He, too, was baffled.

Fabio's dinner was a tremendous success. Even the children asked for second helpings of the rabbit. Robert asked whose recipe had been used for the delectable rabbit. Giullietta gave the credit to Fabio. Rave reviews came from all the governing board members and their wives regarding the dinner.

Dawn came far too quickly the next day. Giullietta was conscious of the hours left for her to talk with Fabio and get back to Tony with a response. She rapidly dressed and waited at the table where they usually met. She could not eat anything while she anxiously waited for him. An hour passed. He and his sons had a battle with an alligator and they had won. They had also secured wild turkeys and quail for the next few evening's dinners.

When Fabio saw Giullietta's expression, he hesitated to inquire what was wrong, but he could not help himself. "Is there something wrong?"

"There is something I must tell you, Fabio."

"What is it?" he asked, suddenly anxious.

"Robert has asked Tony's permission to marry me. Gio and Tony want this to happen. Antonino has taken my father's place and I can't refuse his requests. I didn't want you to hear this news as a surprise."

After a long pause, Fabio extended a sad "congratulations" to her. By now, she had tears in her eyes. She rushed to her wagon. Fabio and the cooking team had to proceed without her.

CHAPTER 50

HEARTACHE

W hen the sun was setting, it was decided that the wedding would be planned for Christmastime. In that way, their church would be ready, and it would be a special first nuptial.

Father Vincenzo asked for the crowd's attention after their sumptuous turkey and quail meal. First, he thanked the cooks for an extraordinary dinner. Everyone clapped, extolling Fabio's name.

Then, the Father began: "I have a very pleasant announcement to make. Robert and Giullietta will be married at Christmastime in our new church!" The congregation clapped enthusiastically. Giullietta excused herself after the speech, claiming she was ill.

That night, after sweet lovemaking, Tony and Gio discussed Giullietta. Robert was a good partner for her and their town. They needed to stay in his good graces. They were confused at her sudden change in heart.

At the same time, Fabio sat by the firelight. For many hours, he attempted to convince himself that Giullietta's decision was the right one and that he had nothing to do with her choice. He needed to find another woman to be his wife and mother to his sons.

He had not slept a wink. He worked on cutting up the alligator so that it could be included in that night's dinner. The tail was a delicacy. Fabio left the parts in an obvious place for the cooks and the hide for Tony, as the community cobbler. Then, he decided to leave to clear his mind, traveling deep into the bayous.

He busied himself with setting traps for snakes. There were plenty of snakes in the area, but he had to be careful of the poisonous ones. *Real ones, not the "official" kind*, he thought. After he captured the serpents, he would skin them and initiate tanning. The skins could be used for shoes, clothing, sacks, hats, hair decorations, and many other items. Tony was interested in purchasing some of them, too, when he had his cobbler shop open. Selling skins had always been a lucrative business for Fabio. All day he kept busy. He ate his meal alone and wondered if anyone noticed.

A day grew into several weeks before he finally returned. During that time, Giullietta fretted about him. She continuously asked his sons when their father would return. Their response was always the same.

"He said he needed to increase his trappings for a greater profit," they told her. "He said he'd return when he had enough money to buy us a house in Little Sicily."

Every morning she waited at "their" table to speak to him. Every morning, he never showed.

Naturally, the days were long and the nights were longer still while she was waiting for Fabio. It was business as usual with the cooks. Every morning they made a nice breakfast for the returning workers, the outgoing workers, hunters, and friends.

Tony dealt with the lumber companies to make a clearing for their farmland and the railroad people to coordinate deliveries. Daniele was in the mud working with his hands giving whatever help he could provide. It was a revelation to see how quickly the new town was being built. The church had structure now, and it was about half finished.

Gio's and Vincenzo's ordering had been exemplary. There was never a waiting period for building materials. The whole congregation worked in their appointed roles, even if it rained or someone had a backache. They all knew they could count on each other. Vincenzo prayed with the leaders that this camaraderie would be unfailing.

One fateful day, while clearing a part of the forest, a tree fell on Dario, the pew maker. His screams were heard throughout the surrounding territory. Father Vincenzo and Gio rushed to the scene.

"What happened?" the Father cried out. He could not understand Placido through his sobbing. An integrated team of workers grunted in their efforts to lift the tree off Dario. It was too late. They had lost a loyal and kind man.

Father directed Remo to carry his friend to their camp. There, Daniele and Rosina could bathe and dress him for the funeral. There was not a dry eye in the group. The men all knew it could easily happen to any one of them. Many skipped dinner, which was a subdued affair. They all prayed with their rosaries for Dario's soul to be safely in heaven.

Dario had always been respected for his stellar carpentry skills. He had already finished building pews, kneelers, and benches for their new church. He had loved God's gift of wood, so his funeral was conducted under the pine trees.

They proclaimed that there would be a sign in the church to acknowledge his major contributions to their community.

Dario had fulfilled a mission in life. Tony remembered what Gio said next to the lake back home, when the beautiful dragonfly was eaten. His life had been meaningful and his mission was completed.

To everyone's surprise, the Jury Commission members, their wives, and some DeRidder workers attended the Mass and spoke sincerely about their friend. That showed what the Triolos always believed, that a positive occurs after a negative.

CHAPTER 51

QUESTIONS

Fabio finally returned. He barely acknowledged Giullietta when he saw her and made it impossible to speak privately with him. When he brought snake meat to the cooks, he explained how they could cook it, but did not participate in the process.

Nunzio, Cuncetta, Giuseppe, Angelina, and a new protégé, Sarafina, took the lead for cooking while Giullietta was doing other things, such as gathering or prepping ingredients or fetching water. After a few cooking lessons with Fabio, Sarafina realized she was becoming increasingly attracted to him. Fabio did not return her attentions for weeks, but eventually, he realized she might be a decent wife for him and mother to his sons. When Giullietta became aware of the situation, she grew frustrated and jealous.

Fabio's sons were very observant. One morning the boys, Stefano, Edoardo, and Pietro brought up the subject of him marrying someone again. They understood their dad's loneliness. Fabio queried his sons about what they thought of Sarafina.

"She's okay," Pietro replied. Fabio repeated his question to the others. Edoardo's response was the same as Pietro's and Stefano's. Then, the subject of Giullietta came up. They all agreed that they thought she was a beautiful lady.

"Too bad she's betrothed to Robert," Stefano said. Fabio changed the topic to what he intended to do with the money he had earned from selling the snakeskins and the fresh game he had caught.

"We have enough money to buy a house now in Little Sicily," Fabio continued. "I think it's time to settle down and have you three attend school. Gio will teach all the students in the fall. When I was younger, I wanted to go to school, but I was never given the opportunity."

"Will we become as smart as Tony and Gio?" Stefano asked.

"Who knows? You may become smarter yet!" his father replied. The boys were excited to go to school, especially with Gio as their teacher.

Dinnertime was fast approaching. The same people sat at Tony's table, except for Fabio and his sons. Instead, they went to sit with Sarafina. Giullietta kept her eyes lowered. Robert was concerned that she was not herself that evening. Suddenly, she stood up and abruptly said goodnight to everyone.

CHAPTER 52

NEWS

The foursome was working alongside the others when a train tooted its whistle, announcing another delivery to the worksite. People not on a work shift went to the delivery zone to help unload several cars. To their surprise, the conductor called Tony and Gio to come forward. He extended his hand and gave them two letters. Corleone, Palermo, was listed as the return address on both. Shocked and joyful, they began to cry. Gio had to sit down immediately, she was so overwhelmed.

It was difficult to read through their tears. Both letters expressed that they were loved and deeply missed. Their parents had written their messages together. One of the important details they related was about the new Sicilian police chief jailing Cosca, Gaetano, Vonzano, and Carlucci mafia members. For the first time, there was peace for the Triad. As a result, the Triolo and Cusimano families were making profits in the sulfur mines and salt fields, just like in the old days. Antonino let out a good loud whistle in response to the news.

Antonino's mother, Anna, was a jokester, and she told her son that she would have sent money if she had not already sealed the envelope. Tony was laughing and crying at the same time. Joking aside, everyone said they would send money if they needed it. It was obvious they did not believe that Tony had found pirates' treasure.

That night, at dinner, residents gathered around a campfire to have Gio and Tony read the news from their letters. When everyone heard about the new Sicilian police chief capturing the mafia members, they jumped up with glee and yelled with joy.

Camaraderie had helped each of them throughout their journey, but it did not replace their homesickness. As people were retiring to bed, there were tears in their eyes.

The next day, the leaders were swamped with people bombarding them to write letters to their families in the Old World. Most were not educated enough to do the task themselves. Placido put each name of the Little Sicily group in a hat. As he drew names out, Gio wrote them down on a list to organize when each individual would work with one of the team members. This plan pleased everyone. If the leaders each wrote one letter a day for their friends, it would take them fifteen days. They would write more per day, if they could, but there was much work to do in Little Sicily.

Three weeks into the project, the outside of their church was completed. The inside of the church was next.

Remo and his crew had been building the organ since the first day their project began. It was an amazing accomplishment. Meanwhile, Benito was creating the altar and pulpit per the specifications of Father Vincenzo. In addition, he had created gold chalices and ornate chandelier light fixtures. He supervised the artists who were creating pictures of the Holy Family, the Saints, and the Apostles. Some of the artwork included three-dimensional carvings of the Stations of the Cross.

The time had arrived to install Dario's pews and kneelers. This action was bittersweet. They all knew he was watching them from heaven. Because Benito and Paolo had worked with Dario on this assignment, Daniele requested that they take the lead for the installation.

Roads were the city's next priority. They would be laid with drainage and modern asphalt cement so that in the future, automobiles would be able to drive over them. Asphalt, a product of crude oil, was mixed with sand, gravel and stone. The next step was to heat the asphalt so that it could be mixed with the aggregates, forming asphalt cement.

Forty houses were to be built initially, some to be sold with the profits going to the town, and thirty shops. Farmers had already planted for the season and an enormous yield was expected. The cleared forest land proved to be fertile. Bushels of fresh fruits and vegetables were picked every day. The workers had built corrals and barns for the livestock. They had planned well for the five square miles, and most everything, so far, would be paid for with the papal money and the treasure. Fundraising ideas were being generated.

CHAPTER 53

APPRECIATION

G iullietta had resigned herself to marrying Robert. Some of the seamstresses were beginning to work on a dress for her and her bridesmaids, with veils made from beautiful Sicilian lace. Nino's parents had sent satin for her wedding dress. Seamstresses were even making suits for Robert, Tony, and Daniele. They had already completed the necessary vestments for Father Vincenzo, his altar boys, and for the altar tapestries.

Giullietta and Robert were getting to know one another's likes and dislikes. It seemed they were more alike than Giullietta had previously thought. Gradually, she felt a deeper appreciation and love for Robert. Excitement about the wedding and Robert, in general, was evolving. She found herself looking forward to a life with him. Her mother knew by her letters, hidden from her father, that she was falling in love with him. Her female family members were busy sewing, knitting, and crocheting a sofa cover, blankets, warm socks, sweaters, skirts, and hats for her and her soon-to-be husband. The Mondadi family was poor, but they wanted to send as much as they could for the betrothed couple.

When cooking meals and eating, Fabio conversed with Sarafina. His sons seemed to like her. She had also taken a genuine interest in his Arabian horse. Fabio was more than willing to demonstrate more tricks he had trained the horse to perform. The tricks were a great prelude to music and dancing on Saturday nights.

Robert was a fun dancer. He liked to twirl Giullietta and catch her in his arms. Daniele and Rosina were always in competition with Tony and Gio for the liveliest couple dancing. In between hugs, spins, rotations, and coiling, they would kiss. They also enjoyed dancing with the group when the tarantella music started. The adolescents had quite a range of songs they could sing.

The single women sewed dresses and made men's ties to match. The ties were randomly distributed among the single men. When they found the woman dressed in the same fabric as their tie, they were to ask her to dance. Many couples found their future spouses in this fashion.

CHAPTER 54

CARNIVAL!

Father Vincenzo gave a dispensation to those men who worked on the Lord's Day, because the work had to get done quickly. They would continue until their town was finished. Those not working on Sundays attended services in the beautiful outdoors and said their rosary for a sustainable future.

During one of the Masses, Gio saw a creature she'd never seen before, kind of like a moth, but bigger, buzzing around and inserting a long beak or stinger into some red flowers. She was mesmerized. After Mass, she asked Robert what it was called.

"It not a moth; it is a hummingbird," he said, mildly amused. "It drinks nectar from the flowers and eats tiny insects."

"Ah, like a combination of a bee and a dragonfly," she said.

"Yes, a little," he responded.

Italy did not have any bird like it. "Our lovely Sicily had no hummingbirds that I ever saw," she mused.

Daniele and Rosina joined the conversation. Gio continued expressing her fascination with this tiny bird. Rosina saw it too, and she loved the sight of it. Gio wished that her family was there to see this part of Louisiana's fauna. She shared her story of this miniature bird with Tony when he returned from supervising construction.

Later in the evening, when Tony was able to speak to Daniele in private, he requested that he secretly draw two large pictures of the hummingbird: one for Gio's family, and one for her. Daniele thought it was a great idea. He decided to make three drawings, so Rosina could have one, too.

Their next meeting with the police jury was Monday, with the topic of raising money for their venture. They decided they would put on a *feste* (carnival) and sell food, handmade products, have games, domino tournaments and sell tickets for admission to an opera performance by the adolescents.

Respect for the immigrants grew while they shared information during town meetings. It was decided that the festivities would be scheduled for July 15, which was the *Santa Rosalia* celebration, in honor of the Corleone patron saint. The congregation needed the entire month to gear up for all the things that needed to be done.

The women organized the carnival, because the men were too busy building Little Sicily. Daniele and Rosina orchestrated the committees. The couple met with the groups daily to go over every detail. The festivities would be conducted on the huge ranch that had been created from clearing part of the forest. High temperatures were expected.

Daniele drew posters and hung them everywhere he and Rosina could find. Vincenzo acquainted himself with the Methodist and Baptist ministers, inviting them with their congregations to attend the carnival. Gio asked all the train conductors to encourage their travelers to come to the festival. It would be open almost all day.

More people came than expected. Word had spread to Merryville and beyond, thanks to Daniele and Rosina's work. People came back for seconds and thirds for the food and wine. They commented on how delicious everything was.

The outside music at the ranch stirred people to dance, play cards and games engaging both the adults and the children alike. The singing troupe performed another comical opera, *The Marriage of Figaro* in the DeRidder Opera House. People came throughout the day, and many who'd arrived early stayed until the end. When closing time came, the immigrants stopped the food and activities to clean.

They were delirious with joy. It would be an excellent fundraiser for the construction of the basilica over the next few years. While counting the money, they discovered they had made enough money to complete the homes and other necessities.

While closing up, the sound of a shot and someone yelling "WOPs!" ripped through the happiness. A herd of folks ran away from the danger. Silence. The immigrants said a quick prayer that no one was hurt.

Placido had been shot. The leaders ran to his rescue. Daniele and Rosina examined him and hurriedly took him back to camp. The bullet had hit the center of his chest and he was bleeding profusely.

Daniele rapidly sanitized his tools for surgery.

"I have the ether," Rosnia said. "Just relax, Placido." But Placido was delirious and fought her until the ether finally overtook him.

Daniele dug into Placido's chest to remove the cartridge. It was a risky surgery because there was the possibility of severing an artery.

"Rosina, retract here so I can see the artery better," Daniele instructed.

Vincenzo prayed with and for the good doctor and nurse to succeed. After wrestling with the flesh, Daniele finally removed the bullet.

They breathed a huge sigh of relief, but there was much recovery needed.

Rosina stitched Placido's chest closed and laid large ice packs on the wound. He had lost a lot of blood.

That night, the team took turns watching over him. He was running an elevated fever and his delirium returned. Cold, wet rags were rotated in and out of ice water and placed on his body. Daniele gave him laudanum for the pain. Only time would tell if he would survive. The next seventy-two hours were nearly unbearable. Vincenzo prayed harder than he ever had.

Infection set in and elevated Placido's body temperature. The prognosis was not good. The medical team gave him pain medication every four hours. The men discussed who had shot Placido. Robert joined their conversation. It was the female leader of the criminal band, who had escaped from jail with her cohorts. She had lured the deputy into her cell by feigning illness, knocked him out, and took his gun and keys.

The commission quickly formed a posse and set out to capture the crooks, yet again. Robert was upset that his deputy had failed to keep the villains in jail.

"Do you need more men for your posse?" asked Tony.

"We had thirty volunteers go," Robert replied. "If they don't catch them in the next two days, I'll come to you for more volunteers. In the meantime, continue to care for Placido. We'll get them one way or another."

Later, Gio strongly expressed that if the posse was not successful, she wanted to ride with Tony to find those loathsome creatures. Fabio wanted to go as well, but he didn't want to wait the two days. He thought *Campione* would be the fastest to get to them, so he led the second posse. Others who were not working at the time joined Fabio. They charged forth from the festival grounds. Their mission was clear. The first posse had covered DeRidder thoroughly, so the second group traveled to Merryville.

Fabio suspected the criminals would end up there sooner or later. While hunting one day, he had discovered a shanty deep in the woods outside the town with guns and ammunition. At the time, he thought hunters lived there, but then he remembered seeing a dress on one of the beds. When they arrived there, they found four horses tied up outside. They waited in the forest until dusk to see if any lights would come on in the shack. Sure enough, they did.

Their attack was vicious and direct. The foursome did not know what hit them. Fabio entered with Tony and Gio. She had brought an iron frying pan, and she hit the female on her head, rendering her unconscious. The criminals were all bound around their arms, legs, and feet. As they exited the premises, the villains were tightly strapped to their horses. The posse stuffed their mouths with cotton. Daniele had provided ether to keep them sedated. At the crack of dawn, the posse entered DeRidder with the four bandits.

Unfortunately, Placido had died while they were away. Gio began to hyperventilate and she soon fainted. She had not been feeling well for some time. They used smelling salts to revive her. Weeping had seemed to be the norm for her the last couple of days. Daniele and Rosina prepped Placido's body for the funeral.

The good news was that the circuit judge had been summoned to try the case in court. He was expected the next day.

CHAPTER 55

CONSEQUENCES

The esteemed judge arrived midafternoon the next day and hurriedly convened the court session. The courtroom was packed. He listened to all the testimony. The verdict of the culprits' punishment was hanging, as soon as the court was adjourned, before he left. The people in the courtroom cheered. The perpetrators were restrained, lifted onto horses, and guided to nooses hanging from some trees. The knotted ropes were fastened around their necks.

Robert shot a gun into the air; consequently, the horses reared up and galloped away, and the crowd could hear the crack of the theives' neck bones as the slack fell out of the ropes. Their faces turned vibrant red and purple; the veins in their faces popped out and their eyes bulged from their sockets. Those who had never seen a hanging before were shocked at the sight.

~ ~ ~

Now the community members had to turn their attention to Placido's funeral. Upon the completion of the rosary, the dirge was sobering. The Requiem (Funeral) Mass would take place the next morning. The immigrants and many of the townspeople silently gathered at the church to join in prayer.

After the extravaganza of the carnival, more people became accustomed to the Italians. Thus, there was a large crowd to honor Placido and his many contributions to Little Sicily. A heartwarming eulogy was delivered by Daniele and Rosina, who had been at his side when he had taken his last breath. They felt it was their responsibility to describe how brave he had been when he was fighting for his life.

Mourners shared many stories about his role with Captain Scardino and the capture of the mafia men on the ship, among other remembrances. It was a stately funeral. After the burial, everyone was invited to share a meal.

It was becoming increasingly obvious to the immigrants that life is fleeting and it is necessary to do one's best while here on Earth. As God-fearing and proactive people, they had decided what they wanted to do in their lives in order to make it meaningful. They knew that God chose them to build Little Sicily. Placido had known he wanted to be an organizer. He had accomplished establishing the city. That was enough.

CHAPTER 56

JUBILATION

The weather after the funeral seemed to be hotter and more humid each day. Tony noticed that Gio was exhausted most of the time. She blamed the heat. She wanted to go to bed earlier each night. Just about everyone else was up when she finally awoke in the mornings. She visited with Daniele to explain her circumstances.

"Obviously, Gio, you're with child," he said.

She could not believe her ears and left to find Tony, who was working in the church. She ran to him and blurted out her good news. He hugged her, spun her around, and whistled with happiness.

"What a perfect place for you to tell me we are having a baby! God has already blessed this child. When?" Tony inquired.

"Daniele thinks, according to when my symptoms of fainting and fatigue began, that I'll deliver next April."

"Fantastic!" he said. "Our child will be an Easter baby!"

When dinnertime came, Vincenzo asked for everyone's attention.

"We have a blessed announcement to make. Gio is pregnant and will deliver next April." Everyone cheered happily.

~ ~ ~

Back in Corleone at Sunday's Mass, Father Primo informed the congregation about what was happening in

DeRidder. Everyone in Palermo knew Tony, Gio, Father Vincenzo, Daniele and their mission. They were anxious to be updated.

"My friends have succeeded!" the priest said. "Cardinal Cusimano will be leaving for Louisiana in a week to consecrate the new church. They've named it *Santa Rosalia*.

The faithful stood and applauded uproariously, for what they considered to be a miracle. They could only imagine how difficult the team's task was in a new, foreign world.

"And Gio's with child!" he said. "Blessed be!"

After Mass, the parishioners planned a party for Cardinal Cusimano before he was to depart. They decided to make the cardinal's favorite dish: beef lasagna and meatballs made with beef and pork. He also liked wild boar salami and duck prosciutto with garlic bread. Of course his favorite, cannoli, would be the dessert.

The cardinal was excited about the voyage. In Gio's letter, she had recommended what food he should take with him, and women of the congregation would see to it that he had enough to sustain him. She had also warned of potential dangers. Captain Scardino would talk to him more in depth on the ship.

The church women scurried to pack his vestments, the wine, chalice, unleavened bread, and the incense burner. Bishop Giorgio Lucchessi had sent him a large gold crucifix for the new holy site. The Pope had sent ornate statues of the holy family and *Santa Rosalia*. Personal items from the Cusimano family were also being gathered to be shipped along with him. Cardinal Cusimano would supervise all of the products, and Captain Scardino would help.

Anna, Josephina, Maria, Isabella, and others with the Triolo, Lorenzo, and Cusimano ladies, made clothes for both men and women for all different occasions, including underwear and nightclothes. Reams of lace, blankets and household items were sent. Beautiful materials, such as silk, were wrapped carefully. They sent many other essentials, such as sewing needles, thread, buttons of all shapes and sizes, crochet needles, knitting needles, and pictures of and patterns for fashion designs. Instruments were also included, such as reed flutes, drums, horns, *pistolatas*, an accordion, Jew's Harps, and harmonicas. Baby clothes and cradles had been made by the female family members, in preparation for this day, even though they hadn't known for sure when the cardinal would be traveling.

Tony's mother, Anna, had started crocheting two huge tablecloths and twenty matching napkins as soon as they had left on their voyage. Gio's mother had sent a handmade jeweled tablecloth for Gio. The tablecloth would become a treasured family heirloom. Squared off ravioli rolling pins, a marble mortar and pestle for making pesto, and a large strainer were also included among the gifts. Both the Triolo and Cusimano families sent assorted tools they thought the new congregation could use. Three families had built a large wine press and fashioned a dozen wine barrels out of the finest oak that they could secure; of course, they were not empty.

"That should give them a good start," the men said.

Family members preserved foods they knew were Gio's and Tony's favorites. Villagers wanted to send remembrances, as well. Zinfandel, Merlot, and Cabernet grapevines were sent in baskets, to replenish the wine barrels. Fruit and tomato seedlings were carefully wrapped and sent like the grapes. Prize-winning Arabian stallions and geldings were to find a new home in America. They were descendants of Campione's and Anna's beauty, Precious. The ship was going to be packed to full capacity.

~ ~ ~

A week later after Mass, aromas whirled through the air, telling the village it was time to attend the meal and extend prayers for Cardinal Cusimano. Music played as they started eating the appetizers. The church's choir sang. When the singing stopped, Bishop Giorgio Lucchessi bid farewell to the holy man. Due to the early departure of the boat the following morning, the cardinal went to bed at dusk.

At four in the morning, the cardinal left the rectory, finding members of the congregation waiting for him outside. They wanted to escort him to the ship. Some walked; some rode horses. Lilting voices rose to the heavens as the cardinal boarded the vessel. The group shouted, *"Buon Viaggio!"* ("Have a great trip!") When the captain gave the order to push away from the shore, the church bells rang. The crowd watched the ship until people could no longer see it on the horizon.

CHAPTER 57

PROGRESS

The one-room schoolhouse took a great deal of time for Gio to organize while it was being built, as she had to order books and supplies. Paolo and the carpenters worked feverishly to construct a teacher's desk and thirty student desks.

Daniele's and Rosina's home was an early build on the priority list, so there could be a place to see patients and set up the medical clinic. Many instruments and supplies had to be ordered, so it would take them more time to have the clinic completely ready. Rosina also arranged a small place to put the sewing machine, material, and thread.

The next big surge of energy went into building furniture, especially beds. Families who were part of the original traveling community received a free home for all their hard work and dedication through every step of the trip. The materials were paid for and they all shared their labor to erect them. The leadership team members' homes had four bedrooms, a front room for conducting business, and an indoor bathroom. Most of the other homes had two or three bedrooms and a bathroom. Every home had the modern additions of running water and electricity, which was so unlike what they'd left in the Old World, and each had a different façade.

After everyone had moved into their homes, construction continued on ten houses to be sold to continue to fund the town. One house was for Fabio and his three sons. Some of the Police Jury Commission families quickly bought up the last few homes. When everyone had settled in, Antonino and Giovanna set up the grocery and supply store. Being a shoemaker, Antonino also had a cobbler's area, which fulfilled a promise to his father.

Life was changing in every way. Each stride toward progress was greeted with excitement and happiness. Their lives were becoming better than they had ever thought possible. The cardinal would be astounded at their superior vision and accomplishments, especially because they had happened in such a short amount of time.

Progress was constant. September came and went. The church was to be dedicated to *Santa Rosalia* on November 1, All Saints' Day, 1906. Vincenzo was expecting Cardinal Cusimano to officiate the sacred ceremony. Gio could not wait to see her uncle.

Knowing that the cardinal was coming, Daniele finally finished the three paintings of the bird with which Gio was so enamored. The day before the cardinal's arrival, Daniele presented these paintings to Gio and Rosina. Both squealed and bounced with happiness. The colors were so vibrant. He had added flora and other fauna to depict where the birds were settling. In that way, the families back home would have a sense of their new land. Gio was so excited that her uncle would be able to bring it back home.

Being blessed with the cardinal's presence, Robert and Giullietta scheduled their wedding three weeks earlier than they had originally planned, in order to have Cardinal Cusimano perform the ceremony while he was there; consequently, the sacrament of marriage was scheduled for late November. The church was ready for the event.

CHAPTER 58

MARVEL

C ardinal Alberto Cusimano and Captain Marcello Scardino became great friends while on their journey. The captain shared stories about Tony and Gio and how they demonstrated the Lord's work. Deporting Maximiliano and his mafia followers was one of the best things Scardino had ever done. The cardinal congratulated Captain Scardino, which meant a great deal to him, not only because he was his friend, but also because he was a cardinal.

Landing in the New World and going through immigration was much easier than expected for the cardinal, and it passed without incident. He'd made sure his station in life was clear by his appearance, which likely helped. His arrival in first class and stately demeanor added to their respect for him. The foursome was waiting for Alberto on the other side of the building. They had so much to share. Eight weeks would not be nearly enough time together.

As their wagons arrived in Little Sicily, the cardinal and the captain were both speechless. *So modern*!

Father Vincenzo wanted his Eminence to see the church first. He would not know what the Pope, bishop, families, and Sicilian villagers had sent until everything was unpacked.

Cardinal Cusimano was very impressed at the speed they erected the first wooden church. He knew that the basilica would take a few years to build, because of it being a masonry structure and the engineering work to build the dome; but, the wooden church was the first step in expanding Catholicism in America. He was so proud of everyone. He only wished that the families and villagers back home could see what he was seeing. Pictures would be taken on consecration day. His arrival party was planned for the next evening.

The cardinal awoke the next morning with the chirping of the Louisiana bird species. The surrounding forests commanded freshness to the air.

"God is good," were his first words when he greeted Tony and Gio.

The cooks anxiously awaited the cardinal and captain at the breakfast table. Both men ate until they thought they would burst. Neither had tasted the New World Cajun herbs used to prepare the newly laid eggs and bacon. The open-air oven had baked the bread to perfection and freshly churned butter melted on the hot loaves.

"My heavens," exclaimed Cardinal Cusimano. The captain joked that he was never going to leave.

Tony spoke up. "You haven't experienced anything yet! Wait until tonight. The cooks and bakers have been preparing for your arrival all week."

Electricity, running water, an indoor gas stove, and beautiful cypress floors and walls in the rectory were almost overwhelming to the cardinal. He had never seen such luxurious wood before. It was varnished to a high polish and he could see his face in the brilliance. The woodworkers had designed furniture for each room.

Vincenzo was antsy to have the cardinal visit the inside of the church during the daytime, so that is what they did next. The rectory was attached to the church so that Father Vincenzo would not get wet when it rained.

The group went through the large hallway to see the house of God. The altar was the ultimate accomplishment. Its legs were gold statues of saints. They upheld the huge carrera marble top with their hands and arms. The masterpiece had been designed by Vincenzo and executed by Benito. Behind the magnificent altar was a beautiful triptych, and alcoves had been prepared to showcase statues of the holy family and the saints.

Electric chandeliers studded the ceilings, dripping with crystals and beads. When Father Vincenzo hit the lights, everyone gasped with delight. People back home would be so amazed.

The walls displayed the three-dimensional stations of the cross, and Daniele explained the unfortunate set of circumstances that had led to Dario's death as they examined the pews. The floors were identical to the rectory floors, with the same high gloss, and they moved down the central aisle. Close to the main entrance, Vincenzo showed off a magnificent painting of the Last Supper. Benito applied the final gold leaf accents to the frame as they toured. All the elegance would be brought to the basilica when it was ready.

The cardinal said it would be an honor for him to consecrate this awe-inspiring holy place. The team knew he would be generous with his description when he reported back to the Sicilians and the Pope.

Late afternoon arrived quickly. Touring the homes and businesses, as well as formal introductions to the Police

Jury Commission, would occur the following week. It was time to get ready for the cardinal's party.

~ ~ ~

Gio and Rosina organized a procession to greet the cardinal. Little girls with flowers in their hair led the lavish procession. Adolescents and operatic singers were next, intermittently singing arias from various operas. Traditional Italian and religious songs were also sung, accompanied by lovely music. Religious, Italian and American flags brought a festive mood to the party which had been created to symbolize the Vatican, the Pope, Sicily, Palermo, Corleone, the United States, and Little Sicily. Last, the devoted community builders paraded by, to much applause from the cardinal and captain.

A full program had been planned for after dinner, but first, the long buffet tables had been filled with delicious food, including various kinds of barbequed game, pasta of all kinds, and bountiful fresh fruits and vegetables from their new land. The meat was topped with unusual sauces that the cooks had learned from the Americans. A myriad of sweet dishes waited at the end of the table. But first, Cardinal Cusimano led the congregation in a prayer of thanksgiving.

When Rosina sat down to eat with Daniele, she accidentally dropped her knife on the ground. Everyone around her cat-called; one of their superstitions was that if someone dropped a knife, it meant a mysterious man was coming. Then, they all laughed and continued eating.

Because Gio knew that her uncle really loved cannoli, she had personally prepared his favorite kind with a delicate dough cylinder and chocolate filling. He smiled broadly while indulging in his niece's delicious dessert. The entertainment also pleased him greatly. The singers of the arias had magnificent voices. The Italian National Anthem and the United States' National Anthem ended the program.

Just then, a crowing of cocks was heard. If crowing occurred during a party, it was interpreted as a bad omen, such as death. The correct "counter" to the superstition was to not eat for the next twenty-four hours. Giullietta joked that she was glad it had happened after their party; otherwise, they would not have had the pleasure of this grand dinner.

CHAPTER 59

SETBACK

The community had prepared to accept the delivery of the gifts from Sicily and stored the commodities in a large warehouse. A party was planned after all the boxes had been organized, stored, and all the animals had been shepherded. Everyone could hardly wait to see everything, even Cardinal Cusimano. Immediately after breakfast, the community gathered in front of the warehouse. They began with a prayer of thanksgiving led by the cardinal.

One entire section of boxes held religious gifts. Onlookers marveled at everything, but the Arabian horses and the exquisite religious articles especially fascinated the congregation. When Gio saw the female Arabian horse, she squealed with delight. The horse was a very shiny dark gray with white socks on her ankles. Her tail was regal and exceptionally long, as was her mane. There was a flash of intelligence in her eyes when she looked at everyone.

"She is yours," Tony said. "What will you call her?"

"I'll have to observe her before I decide," Gio replied.

Fabio volunteered to train Gio's new young filly.

The crowd was impressed with the thoughtfulness of all the donors. How could they ever return the favor?

All the women, especially Giullietta, were amazed when the handmade lace was lifted out of the container. Her wedding was in three weeks. At the sight of the lace, multiple ladies offered to create her veil. Never had she dreamt that her accoutrements would be so gorgeous. Robert was radiant that she was so happy.

While everyone was indulging in the fanfare, someone wildly screamed, "Fire! Fire!" The group was caught off guard. The leadership team ran toward the fire. Everyone else followed.

"Oh my God!" screeched Vincenzo.

Their church, rectory and several houses were on fire, including Daniele's and Rosina's, and Giullietta's and Robert's and Tony's and Gio's. Buckets of water were quickly secured from nearby homes, and the workers began to put the church fire out first. Someone ran downtown to alert the fire department to come with the horse-drawn pump truck. Under their breath, everyone prayed to save their church and the residences.

Giullietta called for Robert. No one knew where he was. A crowd went searching for him. After half an hour, they found him in his home, burned alive. Giullietta was hysterical. He had fiercely labored to save their home. A huge piece of lumber had pinned him down and crushed him. But he had a bullet lodged in his head, too. With that discovery, she fainted. In a few minutes Daniele and Rosina had revived her with smelling salts.

When the leadership group had gathered their wits, they began asking questions. *Did someone not want Robert married to Giullietta?*

"Did anyone see who set the church or residences on fire, or anyone unfamiliar around the church?" Tony began. "If so, what did they look like?"

Fabio's youngest son, Edoardo, spoke up. He said that he had seen five familiar men who delivered the goods from Corleone, but the rest of the men he had not recognized. With that information, the foursome and volunteers decided to set out for Merryville. The arsonists likely would have left town as quickly as possible, but wouldn't have gotten terribly far. The munitions from Palermo had been delivered at the perfect time. Gio would not let Tony leave without her and he didn't have time to argue. Rosina jumped in their wagon with a medical kit as they crossed her path.

CHAPTER 60

ACTION

Tony, Captain Scardino, and the rest of their group rode fiercely into Merryville, searching for Sheriff Michael Brown. The leadership team had met the sheriff when they were passing through town on their way to Little Sicily. The deputy explained that the sheriff and his volunteers were in pursuit of a handful of criminals, at a ranch house located south of town.

The group took off in that direction. The sheriff and posse had been in a firefight for a half hour by the time Tony and the group arrived. The sheriff was immediately informed about all the wicked events that had occurred in Little Sicily.

"Back me up here, boys." he requested.

He suggested they throw fireballs at the house to force the renegades outside, at which point they could capture them.

Twelve men rushed out of the burning house, coughing and having trouble seeing, with their hands up. But one of the villains had hidden a gun under the back of his pants. When the attention was no longer on him, he shot the sheriff in the neck.

One of the volunteers angrily shot the vile man three times, making sure he was dead. Daniele and Rosina leapt into action to try and stop the sheriff's bleeding and gestured to Gio to help them. The firefight continued out in the open, and several more outlaws were taken down. Finally, the immigrants and lawmen had the upper hand, disarmed the remaining criminals, and tied them up.

The medical squad put the sheriff on a horse, with Daniele seated behind him, and he and the ladies rode back to Merryville.

Tony addressed the group, "Who's in charge here?" but no one would respond. "Who's the mastermind?" So, one of the deputies stood one of the men up and pointed his gun at the man's genitals. Again, Tony asked his question. The fiend gestured that the leader was still inside.

Tony, Nunzio, Captain Scardino, and two deputies bounded inside, weapons up.

They could not believe their eyes. "Maximiliano!" gasped Tony. He was sitting in an overstuffed chair and looked relaxed, oblivious to the smoke filling the room from extinguishing the small fires. A damp handkerchief tied around his nose and mouth kept him from coughing.

Captain Scardino just about lost his mind. "What the devil! How—?"

Max just looked at him smugly.

The immigrants knew. How did you do anything in the Old Country? Threats and cash: it was a universal language, especially if you had enough of it. Max had more than enough.

"I don't care how you're here or who you are," a deputy said, putting his gun in Max's face. "You're coming with us."

The second deputy roped him up to the chair, back, arms, and legs, and the five hauled Fortunati out of the house, chair and all. Max was an abdicated "King" on his "throne."

A horse team and wagon pulled up, undoubtedly sent by Daniele, Rosina, and Gio, to gather up the criminals to haul them back to jail.

"You'll *all* hang if the sheriff dies," the deputy said. "That is, *if* you make it to court. It's three days until the judge arrives."

They stuffed the bound prisoners inside and hitched the chair to the back of the wagon, to drag Max behind it, a little less dignified on his "throne."

~ ~ ~

Back at the jail, the thieves were deprived of food and water. Each man was questioned separately and whipped when he did not respond. After a while, they gave up on the men because they knew Miliano was the one who had all the answers. Because Nunzio, Captain Scardino, and Tony knew the ringleader, they were invited to take the lead with his interrogation.

"Why did you follow us here?" Tony began.

"My *connazionali* (countryman)," he said. "Such a lovely town you're starting in Little Sicily. I'm here to start a new life in America, just like you."

"Who's behind you, pulling your strings?"

"I'm an independent businessman," he said, "branching out."

"You're getting nowhere, Tony," Nunzio said. "Go and get my butcher's knives."

At first, everyone thought Nunzio was making empty threats. Tony played along. Nunzio started.

"An eye for an eye, a tooth for a tooth. How about a finger for every unanswered question?"

A deputy entered the room with the announcement that the sheriff had died and that the fires were just about under control. He handed Nunzio a bowie knife.

"So much damage to such a lovely church, tsk, tsk," Max said, feigning concern.

~ ~ ~

All of Tony's blood fell from his head to his feet and he had to grab the wall to keep from toppling over.

"Our church," he said, out of breath. "What do you know about our church?" *Max was behind the church burning?*

"I find it interesting that you fight fire with fire," he said. "Mia *compatriota (neighbor)*."

The room spun for Tony.

"Our church!" Tony shrieked. His sole ambition for nearly six years was destroyed in an instant at *this* man's hands?

"I don't have my whetstone," Nunzio said, "and dull knives hurt much more when they cut you."

Tony needed to leave. He felt like there wasn't any air left in the room. He staggered toward the door.

"Captain," Nunzio said, "move that rope so I can get at his right fingers." The captain complied.

Tony returned and asked, "Why did you do this?" Tony demanded of the prisoner. "Our homes! Five years of our lives! For what?"

No answer.

Nunzio came down swiftly with the knife and chopped off Max's right index, or trigger finger. He wouldn't be shooting a gun again.

To everyone's surprise, there were two screams, Miliano's and Tony's. Miliano's right hand, now exposed, showed off his serpent ring. A Mafia murderer had dropped a serpent ring on the floor during the struggle with his grandparents. His father had shown him, many years before. Tony fell to the floor. Captain Scardino helped him out of the room.

"Who are you working for?" Nunzio repeated. "Who ordered you to do this?"

Still there was no reply.

Next, Nunzio chopped off his right thumb. He wouldn't ever even hold a gun with that hand again. Maximiliano screamed loudly enough for the other men in their cells to become frightened.

"You must be stupid or promised something of great value for your silence," Nunzio said.

A large pool of blood gathered at Maximiliano's feet. It had penetrated his shoes, socks, and the cuff of his pants.

Nunzio cut off the other three right fingers.

He soaked up the blood with Max's jacket and fedora, then used the blood to paint his face with devil symbols.

"If you do not talk," Nunzio said, "we will crucify you upside down like Saint Peter!"

~ ~ ~

Antonino came back in. He had never seen Nunzio in such a state. "Nunzio, you've gone mad; you must stop this."

"He tried to rob us of the Pope's money!" Nunzio shouted, a wild look in his eyes. "He burned our church! Vengeance for our church!"

"Vengeance is God's, not man's," Tony said

Finally, after losing two thumbs and four fingers, Miliano was ready to give in.

"Fine," Max said. "Fine."

Nunzio lowered the knife.

He had been sent by the Vonzano family, the family that Rosina was betrothed to back in Corleone. They had been watching her for some time before the voyage, to make sure she didn't have any other suitors. Maximiliano and his goons came to destroy Rosina's marriage and her life by murdering her husband. He just had shot the wrong man. The leader? Mayor Niccollo Albanesi.

Their last question was what the Vonzanos had offered him as an incentive. By now, in a sweaty half smile, Maximiliano answered.

"Wealth, soldiers, trained Arabian horses, pigs, cows, goats, sheep, wine, and whatever else I wanted to set me up as the Don of the New World."

"This new country would've given you all that and more through honest work," Tony said.

"Why work hard when you can get it the easy way?" replied Maximiliano.

"Instead, you chose to burn in hell," retorted Tony. "What a price!"

Captain Scardino yelled for the deputies. "Take this man away!"

CHAPTER 61

RECOVERY

Giullietta was recovering in the clinic when the group returned. In Daniele's and Rosina's absence, Cuncetta and Vincenzo had cared for her. Gio and Tony went to see her. They assured her that in time, God would heal her. Daniele and Rosina took over her care after thanking Cuncetta and Father Vincenzo for their help.

Tony and Gio excused themselves to hold a community update meeting. Special laudations were given to Nunzio and the Merryville sheriff. All who had participated were commended by the leadership for their valor.

Tony asked for a progress report on the damage. The battle with the fire had lasted until sunrise. They had saved about half the church, and only two of the houses had been seriously affected. Daniele's and Robert's homes, unfortunately, were completely destroyed. The rectory and Tony's house were about a quarter destroyed.

Paolo and Benito had gathered their construction group to determine what supplies would be needed for the repair work. They already knew what they would need for the demolished houses; it was the church reparations that they found more difficult. Nevertheless, they had faith in Paolo.

By evening, they had a complete list. They ventured to New Orleans the next day to ensure that they could obtain the materials. At the first spark of sunrise, the builders were loaded up with travel supplies and money from Vincenzo. If they did not stop and took turns driving the wagons, they could get the supplies and be back in ten to fourteen days. Fabio and *Campione* would race ahead and order the necessary materials, so that when the construction workers with the wagons got to New Orleans, everything would be ready for transport. It was a marvel to witness Fabio and *Campione* in an elegant, lightning-fast gallop.

Cardinal Cusimano would stay longer than planned, so that the church could be consecrated when repairs were completed. Meanwhile, the gifts from Corleone had been inventoried and organized, and distribution of parcels sent to specific people had been completed. The leadership group would need to decide what was to be distributed and to whom of the remainder. Those who had lost their homes would be first. Father Vincenzo and Cardinal Cusimano had organized all the religious items. They planned to give the team a tour of the supply warehouse the next morning.

Tony and Gio were absolutely exhausted. When in bed, he expressed the fear he had felt for her and their unborn child, going on the trip.

"I truly appreciate that you supported me to go," she told him. "I was nearly out of my mind with worry after what happened to you the last time you left me. You are my pillar of solace," Gio said.

"I know exactly what you mean," Tony said sadly. "You are mine, too."

Very softly he rubbed her tummy and said to the baby, "We love you already. We'll work hard to provide you with an education and a good life."

He began singing a love song to Gio and "little Tri-olo." While rubbing her tummy, little Triolo turned in her womb, responding to the song. When Tony finished, he gently kissed Gio's tummy. She felt so safe and loved.

"Gio, my darling, now you are a pillar of life to me. Thank you for having my baby!"

"There would be no living if you weren't here to love and support me," whispered Gio. She thought of her parents missing the birth of their first grandchild and cried herself to sleep.

~ ~ ~

The next morning, the couple toured the warehouse full of gifts. Vincenzo took charge and checked off each item on the list as he explained it. It took nearly all day to review the imports. Vincenzo kept a little secret to tell Tony later.

Gio wanted to be there when Fabio was training her new horse, so she could bond with her beauty.

After the tour, Gio went to help with the lunches. Vincenzo asked Tony to stay behind so that they could talk.

"Your family is so wonderful!" he began. "They asked in their letter that you give the last pieces of the pearl set to Gio, a ring and bracelet."

When Gio saw the heirlooms, she began to weep. These articles had been in the Triolo family for many, many years. She assured Tony that she would take excellent care of them. She did not have to say that; Tony knew she would.

Dinner came and went, allowing Gio to rest. She seemed so tired since she had found out she was pregnant. They fell asleep in each other's arms.

The next day, Gio anxiously wanted to work with Fabio to begin getting acquainted with her gorgeous filly. She brought a bunch of freshly picked carrots for the horse's snack. From then on, every morning Gio repeated the ritual. Her horse seemed royal in her ways, but she was gentle and respectful during the training sessions.

Campione watched, too. In fact, he was part of the training. The filly seemed to emulate many of the things that he did. After two weeks, Gio couldn't wait any longer to mount the beauty. The horse perceived that she must be placid and good-natured when her owner was in the saddle. She had the knack to prance excellently, and if one observed closely, one could swear she smiled while Gio was riding her.

The horse and Gio knew they were meant for each other. One morning, after feeding the filly freshly picked carrots, Gio announced to Tony and Fabio that she thought this magnificent animal should be named *Regina* (Queen). In the next year, *Campione* and *Regina* would be bred to have foals.

~ ~ ~

Sitting in the DeRidder courtroom two days later, wisdom prevailed over the jury. Seven remaining crooks were sentenced to the jail in New Orleans for ten years. Maximiliano received the death sentence as the ringleader in charge of Robert's murder, as well as the henchman who murdered the sheriff. A witness also testified that Maximiliano had also murdered a Creole.

"This is justice in action," snarled Nunzio.

Nunzio requested to be part of the legal escort to New Orleans. He wanted to ensure their community that he had witnessed the extermination of Maximiliano once and for all.

"Be safe," Tony told him.

Giullietta did not have the energy to be happy about the verdict.

CHAPTER 62

GIFTS OF LOVE

The builders returned with supplies from New Orleans. While they had been gone, the men who remained in Little Sicily had worked hard to clear out the burned items in the church, rectory, and the homes that had been damaged. The day after their arrival, the around-the-clock shifts began again on construction. Within four weeks, the house of worship had been rebuilt.

The large statues of the Holy Family and *Santa Rosalia* were put into place. Religious pictures and decorations adorned the lovely church. The gold crucifix sent by the bishop beautified the altar. Artifacts, such as a chip of bone from *Santa Rosalia*, had been placed in a small Baroque box and then locked into a small chamber in the altar. Traditionally, each basilica and church had a sliver of bone from a saint for whom the place of worship was named. Exquisite fabrics rested on the altar. Vincenzo's pulpit had been decoratively fashioned out of cypress. It was a sight to behold. Their original date for the consecration had been delayed by only a few weeks. The sacred ceremony was scheduled for two weeks from Sunday.

The Methodist and Baptist pastors, along with the Police Jury Commission members, came to visit. They were fascinated as though they were walking into a museum. They admitted it was breathtaking and inspirational. All had been invited to the upcoming ceremony. As the project was near completion, the other structures that needed repair were being addressed.

Even the cooks were exhausted. When not preparing a meal, they farmed, so, the meal was simple: pasta and fresh vegetables. Unbeknown to Giullietta, Fabio had asked permission from Tony and Father Vincenzo to marry Sarafina. They had discussed nuptials on several occasions, and her response had always been positive. He wanted Father Vincenzo to announce it at dinner.

Fabio was prepared. A sparkling diamond ring had caught his attention when he had gone to New Orleans for their supplies. In the middle of dinner, Father Vincenzo asked for everyone's attention. The crowd became silent. Vincenzo cleared his throat and began: "Fabio has asked permission to marry Sarafina." Cheers could be heard all around the forest. They wanted to know what date they had chosen.

The bride-to-be shouted out: "A week after Easter Sunday!" Fabio grinned.

"Well, there you have it," the gentle Father said. Congratulations came from everyone. Even Fabio's three sons were delighted. Sarafina kissed Fabio in front of everyone.

It was too much for Giullietta, who feigned illness and ran away from dinner. Slowly, as Tony and Gio had promised, God was allowing Giullietta to recover from her loss of Robert, but Fabio's marriage felt like a second murder for her. Even though she had grown to admire and love Robert, he had not been Giullietta's first, true love.

Campione did not want to be excluded from what was happening. He sensed that it was something happy for his master; he went toward Fabio and stole the hat from his head. This trick had the group roaring with laughter. Being the obedient horse that he was, when Fabio called him back, he listened. His master told him to return the hat. He put the hat on Tony. More laughter. *Campione* knew exactly what he was doing. When cajoled again, he put the hat on Sarafina.

"What a brilliant horse," said Daniele.

For the last encore, *Campione* rested the hat on Fabio's head and took a bow. He received a standing ovation. That story would be repeated many times in the years to come.

CHAPTER 63

LETTERS FROM LITTLE SICILY

Meanwhile in Sicily, Francesco and Anna invited everyone for dinner when they received mail from Tony and Gio. Both letters thanked everyone for the fabulous imports. The letters had similar content, but Gio's was far more sentimental. She assured them that her pregnancy was going fine. She was exuberant about the crocheted blankets and pillows that had been made for the crib. Included in her words was news about upcoming events, such as the consecration of their church, future marriages, and various other plans. In great detail, she described their newly built church, and she also sent a few Cajun and Creole recipes with the appropriate herbs for them to try.

Her expressions of delight pleased them when she spoke of *Regina* and what she was being trained to do. Happily she described how she brought fresh carrots to her every morning.

"We love each other very much," she wrote. Besides the heirloom jewelry, *Regina* was the greatest gift of all.

Tony informed his family that Mayor Niccollo Albanesi Vonzano (his full name) was truly the head of the Vonzano mafia family and what he had ordered Maximiliano to do. He explained the details and requested that they share this information with the new Sicilian Chief of Police. "I was surprised how well Niccollo hid his real identity."

When General Provenza received the information, he immediately organized a posse and approached Niccollo. Not anticipating the general entering his office, he had not attempted to hide the serpent ring. That was the only proof the general needed to arrest him.

Tony's letter explained the fire and the events that had followed. He assured them that everything was now under control. In fact, one of their friends had just returned from New Orleans to confirm that Maximiliano Fortunati had been hanged. Nunzio had witnessed the execution. Tony suggested they put the word out in Palermo so that the Vonzanos would know that their miserable plot had failed. Surely, word would quickly reach the Vonzanos, because some of the lesser criminals had been released from prison. Tony added in his letter that their good friend, Captain Scardino, would make contact with them in early summer.

CHAPTER 64

ROOTS

S unday arrived. It was time for the consecration of their church. It had been highly advertised; almost everyone from their community and many from DeRidder attended. Even Papa and Mamma Tucci were invited by Fabio when in New Orleans. They came to see the ceremony. The procession was very long. Some of the smaller religious items were being carried as gifts for their new house of worship. Music flourished and songs were sung in Italian and English. They were getting better at singing the American National Anthem. The Sicilians were so grateful to America for giving them the chance to better themselves and be productive citizens. The ceremony lasted two hours.

After the service, the party began. Some things never get old. Celebrations were part of their way of life. They gave them a sense of pride, belonging, fun, and collaboration. Cardinal Cusimano had been convinced to stay past Christmas.

~ ~ ~

The cardinal was scheduled to leave with the captain in a few days, so they had made the time extra special by planning what would go back to Sicily with them: preserves of fruits and vegetables that were not readily available in Palermo and some gold leaf art pieces for Father Primo's church.

The sendoff was beautiful, and the team stood along the lines of people saying goodbye. Many hugs were shared before they left in the wagon. Gio cried to see her uncle go; he reminded her so much of exalted Corleone and all their family.

The thought of bringing their baby into their new home made them anxious for its birth. Tony wrapped his arms around her to console her, even though he had tears in his eyes as well. Tony and Gio were so thankful to have such loving friends with whom they had made such progress.

After the cardinal's departure, the community focused on constructing Baroque state and public buildings. It was an era that appreciated resplendence for these types of buildings. Being the industrious people that they were, three eight-hour shifts were reinstated. For the next three months, the men continued construction of the town, and the women hustled to plan for the union of Fabio and Sarafina. The handmade lace making up her gown and veil was easy to work with. One of the women had been breeding doves to release into the sky for good luck on their special day.

Unexpectantly, Sarafina received word that her mother was ill and dying. Her father begged her to come because her mother requested that her daughter be with her when she died.

Sarafina apologized to Fabio and the community. Fabio released her from her obligation to marry him. It was a sad farewell, but Sarafina did what her parents requested.

As soon as Giullietta heard the news, she rushed to Fabio. He picked her up and swung her around with a hug.

Fabio told her that she was his true love. Giullietta melted in his arms. She was going to marry Robert because

Tony and Gio wanted it so; but, she told Fabio that he was her first true love.

They asked Father Vincenzo to announce their wedding at the next dinner. Though people were a little surprised, they cheered none the less.

The next day, Giullietta happily planned a five-layer wedding cake to accommodate almost everyone's taste. Each layer would be a different flavor. Chocolate was chosen for the bottom, because it was the largest layer. Next, *zuppa inglese (rum cake)*, then vanilla and strawberry. Last, but not least was the apple cake layer. Between each layer would be alternating bands of raspberry and apricot jam. The bakers had never attempted something quite like this.

The ceremony was scheduled for noon on the Sunday following Easter. It was a lovely day. Fabio and Giullietta rode in an adorned carriage to *Santa Rosalia*. *Regina* now knew some fancy steps, enabling her and *Campione* to put on the show of shows. Many of the people from DeRidder had never seen this type of footwork by a horse pulling a carriage.

Fabio's three sons, along with Tony, Daniele, and Nunzio, greeted everyone at the door and escorted attendees to their seats. The church was packed full, with others waiting outside the door trying to get a peek. Spring flowers graced every nook and cranny. Following the Nuptial Mass, they invited everyone to the reception in their new hall. Surely, the couple's future would be charmed.

In the middle of building, on one of the warm days, Gio was feeling pains, and her water broke. Giullietta ran to find Tony. He was supervising construction. When he saw her rushing toward him with an anxious look, he instinctively knew it was time for the baby. He yelled for Daniele and Rosina to come quickly. In about ten hours, Tony and Gio were the proud parents of Francesco (Frankie) Triolo, the namesake for Tony's father.

Frankie was twenty-one inches long and weighed eight pounds, two ounces. He had lots of black hair on top of his head. His fingers were long, and, thus, Tony hoped that he would one day play an instrument. His skin was light olive, and he had hazel eyes, just like his grandmother, Anna. Frankie had Gio's nose, which was just like her father's.

Word spread quickly. People came to congratulate the happy couple. Immediately, Tony wrote a letter to both families, announcing the news while Gio rested. Fabio mailed it for him.

Frankie was born on a Tuesday, so the Baptism was planned for that Sunday. While Gio sat nursing Frankie, Tony held their hands. He was weeping for the miracle happening before him.

Gio looked up and said, "There would be no living without you, Tony." He could hardly get the words out of his throat to say his vows to his dearest love. "You are the pillar of our family, Tony. I love both of you so much!"

The community prepared for the first Baptism to be performed in their church. Bruno and Josephina were asked to be the godparents, even though they couldn't be present. The baptism is performed as soon after the birth as possible. Traditionally, an unbaptized baby was susceptible to the devil or the evil eye.

Rosina was making Francesco's baptismal dress and hat out of the satin and lace that had come from Corleone. The clothes and shoes from Corleone, Palermo, were divided up after Gio and Tony chose for themselves. Even *Campione* and *Regina* would be adorned with white satin-and-lace bridles and covers under their saddles. Decorative bows and plumes were placed in their manes. The horses both knew that they had to put on their best performance in the processional. The new baby was seen as their royalty because the congregation loved and respected Tony and Gio so much.

By noon, everyone was ready to begin the procession. Gio, Tony, and little Francesco, now being called Frankie, rode in the carriage that Giullietta and Fabio had used when they had been married. It had been painted white, and it was decorated on the sides. Daniele had made a beautiful sign welcoming Frankie into his new family. Long streams of people from Merryville, DeRidder, and Little Sicily walked and sang along the pathway to the church. Small children led the way by dropping flowers on the ground on the pathway of the procession. *Campione* and *Regina* were exactly in tandem as they pranced together.

The highly decorated bronze doors were opened to welcome everyone. These doors had been fashioned after the "Gates of Paradise" at the Duomo in Florence, Italy. There were twenty-eight three dimensional depictions on them. Some were designed to represent activities of Jesus while on earth; there were moldings representative of Adam and Eve and many Old Testament people such as Cain and Abel. There was foliage and fruit outlining the individuals. People marveled at the detail and beauty of the entrance.

Father Vincenzo greeted them at the entrance and slowly led them in the church. At the baptismal font, the priest gently poured water on Frankie's forehead while saying the appropriate prayers. Naturally, Frankie screamed. Even the horses outside were restless when they heard him. Everyone laughed and said the baby had strong lungs.

In the church hall after the ceremony, the party began. People danced and sang joyfully. Tony and Gio danced, while Frankie was passed from "auntie" to "uncle" around the happy crowd. The food was extra delicious because Fabio and Giullietta had planned the menu.

Sharing, caring, and collaboration from everyone was the ideal that came to life on such a special day. The party lasted until the late hours of the night.

When Tony and Gio were in bed after the celebration, they lamented that their families from Corleone had not been there to witness such a beautiful day.

"Oh, Tony, will we ever feel completely at home here?" Gio asked.

The next morning, Rosina, Giullietta, Gio, and Frankie gave Duchess her bunch of carrots. She told her how proud she was of her for working with *Campione*. Somehow *Regina* knew what she was saying, shook her head in acknowledgement, and snorted, smiling all the while. Both Giullietta and Gio got a gentle nudge from *Regina*, who was acknowledging her "partners in pregnancy." More babies were on their way.

Fabio had encouraged the horse to be gentle, which was natural for her. Someday, Gio would be able to ride her with Frankie, too.

~ ~ ~

Other Sicilians from Palermo began arriving in Little Sicily, because Papa and Mamma Tucci from the "Welcome Center" in New Orleans had told new immigrants about what was happening there. Their first experience would be the familiar procession for *Santa Rosalia*. There, they would meet Father Vincenzo and others in the community.

Each of the original twenty immigrant families invited a family or small group of individuals into their homes, and in exchange, the new immigrant men helped construct a large apartment building that would be able to accommodate their group. The new populace was amazed at how things happened so quickly. But the people in Little Sicily had been through just about everything in the past year and a half. A week's respite was given to the newcomers; then, the construction began. The new immigrants helped with the plans.

A few ladies had lived in places other than Sicily when they were young. One lady knew Roman cooking; another cooked Naples' style. It made for a deliciously different *Santa Rosalia* celebration. There was a mix of Roman, Calabrian, Sicilian, American, Creole, and Cajun food. Such a merging of flavors!

The apartments would be finished for the new people by the end of summer, and folks would begin to move into them. Tony and Gio had the grocery and supply store and the shoemaking business to grow. Daniele and Rosina were working on their clinic, with a vision for a hospital. Father Vincenzo's responsibilities were enlarging because the population was increasing, and accordingly, there were more funerals, weddings, and baptisms.

The summer turned into fall. Adorable Frankie crawled and was a good eater just like his grandfather, Francesco. Sophia loved to play with him and they amused each other. One beautiful day, Gio took Sophia, Giuseppe, Angelina, and Frankie to see *Regina*. They were feeding the horses a bunch of carrots. *Regina* wanted more because she was still eating for two. Tony, Frankie, and Sophia played outside the corral while Gio brushed her beauty. The six of them soaked in the sun and fresh air.

Suddenly she heard a familiar voice calling her in the distance. It was neither Tony's nor Daniele's. She listened carefully. Gio thought she was having a daydream. She looked up and saw her parents, Tony's parents, the Soraccos, and the Lorenzos!

"This can't be true," she said. As they got closer, Gio dropped the brush and went running to them. Tears flooded everyone's eyes including Tony's. He had wanted to surprise Gio and he had made arrangements with Captain Scardino before he had left with Cardinal Cusimano to bring their families to America.

Gio laughed and cried so hard that she fainted. Tony swept her up, grandparents gleefully picked up the little ones, and everyone entered their home. Even Father Primo and Bishop Lucchessi were with them. Father Vincenzo anxiously awaited their visit so he could showcase their church, but that could wait until the next day.

Dinnertime was approaching, and the grandparents were "fighting" over who got to hold Frankie and Sophia. The child knew something special was happening, and as a result, he was showing off with Sophia. Giuseppe and

Angelina were so happy that everyone had taken an interest in her, too. After all, they were the only grandparents around to spoil the children.

For dinner there were several types of seafood: mussels, oysters, clams, and shrimp prepared in a variety of ways to be mixed in with several kinds of pasta and either a red or white cheese sauce. The fruits and vegetables were grilled to perfection and the desserts were sublime. The Triad and the priests had not eaten like this since they had been back home in Corleone.

Francesco recognized that all the members of his family had been pillars of a legacy; that their contributions would be added to and sustained in the future for the Triolo family and the world.

Gio could not be happier. She thanked Tony over and over again for bringing all their family to America.

"Would it be all right for us to stay in America, do you think, Gio," her mother teased, "so Frankie could be properly spoiled?"

Gio squealed and embraced her mother tightly.

Bruno, Francesco and Antonino whistled.

La Vita è Bella! (Life is beautiful!). It could not get better than this-or could it?

CPSIA information can be obtained
at www.ICGtesting.com
Printed in the USA
FSHW02n1759280618
49818FS